D0930039

Cultural Democracy,
Bicognitive Development,
and Education

Theodore Lownik Library
Illinois Benedictine College
Lisle, Illinois 60532

Cultural Democracy, Bicognitive Development, and Education

Manuel Ramírez III
Oakes College
University of California
Santa Cruz, California

Alfredo Castañeda
School of Education
Stanford University
Stanford, California

ACADEMIC PRESS   New York   San Francisco   London

A Subsidiary of Harcourt Brace Jovanovich, Publishers

LC
2682
.R35

COPYRIGHT © 1974, BY ACADEMIC PRESS, INC.
ALL RIGHTS RESERVED.
NO PART OF THIS PUBLICATION MAY BE REPRODUCED OR
TRANSMITTED IN ANY FORM OR BY ANY MEANS, ELECTRONIC
OR MECHANICAL, INCLUDING PHOTOCOPY, RECORDING, OR ANY
INFORMATION STORAGE AND RETRIEVAL SYSTEM, WITHOUT
PERMISSION IN WRITING FROM THE PUBLISHER.

ACADEMIC PRESS, INC.
111 Fifth Avenue, New York, New York 10003

United Kingdom Edition published by
ACADEMIC PRESS, INC. (LONDON) LTD.
24/28 Oval Road, London NW1

Library of Congress Cataloging in Publication Data

Ramírez, Manuel, Date
    Cultural democracy, bicognitive development, and
education.

    Includes bibliographies.
        1.   Mexican Americans–Education.   2.   Intercultural
education.   I.   Castañeda, Alfredo, joint author.
II.   Title.
LC2682.R35   371.9'7   74-5699
ISBN 0–12–577250–5

PRINTED IN THE UNITED STATES OF AMERICA

Dedicated to our parents,

Señor Manuel Ramírez, Jr. and Señora Consuelo Sanchez Ramírez
and
Señor Salvador Castañeda and Señora Manuela Ávila Castañeda

Contents

Preface

This book is concerned with how American society can promote and sustain its diversity and be sensitive to individual differences through educational pluralism. By focusing our attention on Mexican Americans, we attempt to formulate a philosophy of education based on our ideas of "cultural democracy." This philosophy serves as the foundation for a new educational policy designed to help children of diverse backgrounds learn effectively. Cultural democracy assumes that a person has a legal as well as a moral right to remain identified with his own ethnic group, his own values, language, home, and community, as he learns of and accepts "mainstream" values.

Two focal concepts are also discussed: bicultural identity and bicognitive development. Many culturally different children have been made to feel that they must reject the culture of their homes in order to succeed in school. As an objective of cultural democracy,

however, bicultural identity includes the ability to function competently in two cultures, to view oneself as belonging to two cultures.

The concept of bicognitive development has emerged from recent research on cognitive style. Two separate and distinct cognitive styles have been identified. Recent brain research suggests
these two cognitive styles may be associated with cerebral hemis-
pheric specializations. Public education in America reflects and
reinforces one cognitive style over the other. Culturally democratic
educational environments would enable children to develop *both*
cognitive styles, to practice cognitive switching, and thereby be
able to meet the diverse demands of life more effectively.

We attempt to show how the philosophy of cultural democracy
can influence policies and practices in education so that the pluralis-
tic character of America is sustained and promoted in our schools.
Through cultural democracy, with the concepts of bicultural identity
and bicognitive development, American education can meet the
demands of future years; meet the needs of all Americans, and help
America utilize the strengths to be found in the individual differences
of its people.

Acknowledgments

The financial support for the research which served as the basis for this book was provided by two grants, one from Project Follow Through, Office of Education, Grant No. OEG-0-70-4939(286) and another from the Division of Bilingual Education, Bilingual Education Act (ESEA Title VII), Grant No. OEG-9-72-0154(280), Project No. 14-0448.

We are indebted to Barbara Goffigon Cox for her many contributions in developing and clarifying essential concepts, as well as organizing and editing the many drafts.

We also would like to thank Professor P. Leslie Herold, Dr. Albar Peña, Elizabeth Keesee, and Janet Macaulay for suggesting valuable ideas which were incorporated into the manuscript.

Many of our students made significant contributions to this book. We are particularly grateful to Mary Lou Dominguez, Tracy Gray, Ray Buriel, and Fred Estrada. We are also thankful to the teachers and administrative staff of the Cucamonga Independent School District and to the staff of the Culturally Democratic Educational Environments model at the University of California at Santa Cruz.

We also wish to express our appreciation to Maria Perez and Rosemary Sedillo Glatt for their help in preparing the manuscript.

1

The Ideology of Assimilation

Introduction

The Mexican American experience in public education reflects a history of neglect culminating in educational attainment figures such as those described by Moore (1970) in her book, *Mexican Americans:*

> Throughout the Southwest the Mexican American adult population was too badly educated in 1960 to participate effectively in modern American society. . . . they attained a median of 7.1 years of schooling as compared with 12.1 for Anglos and 9.0 for nonwhites (adults of 25 years and over). In California the figure was highest, 8.6 years. It Is lowest in Texas at 4.8 years or only slightly better than functional illiteracy. In all states Negroes are better educated than Mexican Americans. (Nonwhite medians are pulled down in New Mexico and Arizona by the large proportion of Indians with extremely low levels of schooling.) Among Mexicans the incidence of functional illiteracy (0 to 4 years of

elementary school) is seven times that of the Anglo population and nearly twice that of nonwhites as a whole [p. 65].

The consequences of educational neglect are also evident at the college and university level. In 1960, some college experience was reported by only 5.6% of Mexican American persons aged 14 or over, while twice as many other nonwhites and four times as many Anglo–Americans reported college attendance. Several excellent publications which further delineate the educational plight of Mexican Americans have recently appeared under the auspices of the United States Civil Rights Commission (1971a,b, 1972a,b, and 1973).

As a distinctive ethnic population, Mexican Americans have been frequently referred to as the "least Americanized" of all America's ethnic groups, "unassimilable," and "foreign." These descriptions are often used as *explanations* for the educational and economic plight in which the majority of the Mexican American population finds itself today.

Social scientists and educators have long viewed the Mexican American population with utter bemusement for its failure to follow the historical patterns of acculturation and assimilation that have been attributed to many other major ethnic groups (for example, Heller, 1971). The sources of the confusion lie in several important historical points. American assimilation ideology has had as its base the phenomenon of *transoceanic* migration. Furthermore, it has been assumed that a prime motivation for this phenomenon was a political one: Peoples migrating from Europe came to America chiefly to escape political oppression and to benefit from the liberties promised by American democratic ideology. Hansen (1948) has suggested that this assumption implied another strong motivation, namely that immigrants desired to adopt American values, customs, and manners.

Frequently overlooked is the fact that the historical reasons for the presence of Mexican Americans in the United States represent an entirely different pattern: Mexican Americans share with the American Indian the experience of conquest and annexation. Thus, by virtue of the Treaty of Guadalupe Hidalgo in 1848, Mexicans residing in the Southwest became American citizens and were guaranteed equal protection and treatment under the American Constitution. The strong cultural and familial ties existing between Mexico and those of Mexican descent residing in Texas, Arizona, New Mexico, Colorado, and California remained strong in spite of this treaty. These strong cultural ties continue to be reinforced to this day by virtue of almost daily migration, geographical proximity, and highly developed communication and transportation technology. Other factors such as institutionally sanctioned discrimination in the economic, political, social, and educational spheres of American life have undoubtedly added to the inability of Mexican Americans to participate in American society more fully. These factors have all contributed to making the Mexican American population appear more culturally distinct from the American mainstream, and it is this distinctiveness that has contributed to the view of Mexican Americans as "unassimilable," "least Americanized," and "foreign."

The Myth of an American National Character

The modern conception of "national character" and motivation for believing in or seeking such a character has its roots largely in the nineteenth century when efforts of nationalities to gain independence, and of imperialist powers to justify their right to rule were fused with racial superiority theory. In its own efforts to gain independence, the United States early evolved a social theory largely intended to create cultural patterns that would produce a distinctly "American" personality—the theory of the melting pot. However, the United States persists, as far as its character as a nation is concerned, as one of the most heterogeneous nations in the world today in terms of its cultural, racial, and social diversity. With the social ferment of the 1960s came critical examination of the role of melting-pot theory as an instrument for the formulation of educational policy and practice.

The melting-pot theory assumes that a sociocultural system can be created on a national scale such that it functions effectively for the majority of the population. Melting-pot theory presumes a monolithic effectiveness in determining the socialization goals and practices of the home, school, and community. Yet the social reality in

the United States is that there exists an astounding array of sociocultural systems.

One of the central themes of this book is that the sociocultural
system of which the child is a product must be clearly understood
if public education is to be effective. A sociocultural system can
be viewed from the cultural patterns or socialization clusters which
produce distinctive modes or styles with regard to (1) communication, (2) human relations, (3) learning, and (4) motivation. American
public education is criticized today for its exclusive reinforcement
of the sociocultural system of the mainstream American middle
class. This criticism was stated forcefully by McDavid (1969) in the
published proceedings of six Head Start Research Seminars held
under the auspices of the United States Office of Economic
Opportunity:

> Our society is a diverse and heterogeneous one, in which we embrace
> a variety of subcultures delineated by ethnic, linguistic, racial, geo-
> graphic, educational, and socioeconomic earmarks. Within each of these
> subcultures, social standards vary, and corresponding socialization
> practices vary. Yet we plan public education as a single, massive, uni-
> form Procrustean institutionalized system of values, beliefs, and habits
> defined according to some stereotype rising magically out of the
> middle-class pillars of society. . . . This, then, is the stereotypical
> target toward which our institutionalized educational system tends to
> socialize all of its participants, regardless of the adult subculture to
> which they are bound, and regardless of the relevancy or irrelevancy of
> these values and habits to each one's own real world [pp. 5–6].

McDavid's comments vividly illustrate the persistence of the belief
in a single, exclusive definition of American character. The influence
of this belief in determining educational policy and practice has
been prominent and pervasive. The differences in the level of educational attainment between children of the mainstream American middle class and children whose cultural backgrounds differ strongly
imply that this viewpoint works against the best interests of public
education. In order to ensure equal educational opportunities for
all Americans, public educational policy and practice must first
weigh two major considerations.

From the perspective of educational policy and practice, first, public education must seek whatever information the social sciences

can provide concerning the different sociocultural systems from which its children come. That is, the schools must seek to discover the unique communication, human–relational, learning, and motivational patterns that are produced in children coming from sociocultural systems different from that of the mainstream American middle class. Second, knowing what these unique patterns are, public education must adopt policies and practices that reinforce or are consistent with these unique socialization patterns.

A Mixed Legacy

The assumptions underlying present-day efforts of American public education to prepare children of ethnic minorities for productive and fulfilling roles in society constitute a mixture of several legacies originating in American social thought concerning assimilation. The mixed legacy, however, can be sorted out into the several major themes of the "melting pot" versus "cultural pluralism." Within the general melting-pot category there are two major variants, i.e., whether the process of melting is to be "permissive" or "exclusive." These will be discussed in the following subsections. Within the cultural pluralists' category, two general themes may also be noted, its mandatory or optional character. These are discussed in Chapter 2.

The Melting Pot

The Permissive Melting Pot

While the *exclusivist* version of the melting pot has probably been the most prevalent ideology of assimilation in America, a competing viewpoint with somewhat more generous and idealistic overtones has had its adherents and proponents since the eighteenth century. Conditions on the American continent were modifying the institutions which the English colonists brought with them. Immigrants from non-English homelands such as Sweden, Germany, and France were similarly exposed to this new environment. Thus, starting with the

French-born writer, Crevecoeur, in 1782, a new social theory—America as a melting pot—came into being. He thought of the evolving American society not as a slightly modified England, but as a totally new blend, culturally and biologically, in which stocks and folkways of Europe, figuratively speaking, indiscriminately (permissively) mixed in the political pot of the emerging nation and melted together by the fires of the American influence and interaction into a distinctly new type, a distinctly American personality:

> I could point out to you a family whose grandfather was an Englishman, whose wife was Dutch, whose son married a French woman, and whose present four sons have now four wives of different nations. *He* is an American, who leaving behind him all his ancient prejudices and manners, receives new ones from the new mode of life he has embraced. . . . Here individuals of all nations are melted into a new race of men [pp. 54–55].

By 1908 the social theory of the melting pot and its goal of a distinctly American character of personality gained such prominence that it served as the theme for an instantly successful play entitled, appropriately, *The Melting Pot,* in which one of the characters exults:

> . . . America is God's Crucible, the Great Melting Pot where all races of Europe are melting and re-forming! Here you stand . . . in your fifty groups, with your fifty languages and histories, and your fifty blood hatreds and rivalries. But you won't be long like that, brothers, . . . God is making the American. . . . the real American has not yet arrived. . . . he will be the fusion of all the races, perhaps the coming superman.

The permissive version of the melting-pot theory presumed indiscriminate biological and cultural amalgamation of northern European populations, and it did serve as a forceful ideological basis for permissive immigration policies during this period. Yet the product of the melting process was left unspecified with one exception: the melted product was envisioned as superior to any of the individual ingredients constituting the mix. Thus the permissive notion of the melting pot clearly embraced a notion of the supremacy of the product. Furthermore, this version of the melting pot omitted from consideration two indigenous peoples, the native Americans and the

Mexicans of the Southwest, as well as that group forcibly brought to America, the black Americans.

By 1916 the superiority of this new blend was being developed by writers of such stature as John Dewey (1916), the noted American educator–philosopher who remarked:

> I wish our teaching of American history in the schools would take more account of the great waves of migration by which our land for over three centuries has been continuously built up, and made every pupil conscious of the rich breadth of our national make-up. When every pupil recognizes all the factors which have gone into our being, he will continue to prize and reverence that coming from his own past, but he will think of it as honored in being simply one factor in forming a whole, *nobler and finer* than itself [p. 140; emphasis added].

Dewey's vision of the superiority of the melted product over the individual ingredients seems easily inferable from his words, "nobler and finer than itself." This statement clearly seems to say that one's own cultural heritage is okay, but when it has blended with others the result is even better. Despite its liberal overtones, the permissive interpretation of the melting pot has carried a hidden message of cultural superiority: The uniquely American cultural form will be better, if not the best. The message to the child who has not yet "melted" is clearly negative—that what he is is not good enough, there is something "nobler and finer."

The Exclusivist Melting Pot: Anglo Conformity

Despite the presence of peoples whose language, customs, and often appearances are different, the cultural and political aspirations and privileges of the Anglo–Saxon Protestant group have been maintained almost exclusively. Through dominance of American institutions with their control of the nation's resources and hence the destiny of the individual, this group has managed to direct the acculturation and assimilation of other ethnic groups. Thus, it has more or less successfully acculturated and assimilated some ethnic minorities, acculturated but not assimilated some, and failed to acculturate or assimilate others.

As long as migration was predominantly from northern Europe, it was assumed that cultural differences in the ethnic groups representing that part of the world would disappear. The process whereby this social phenomenon would take place was acculturation into the Anglo–Saxon cultural ideal. If acculturation was to be completely successful, it would have to proceed both externally (language, heritage, dress, religion, and secular roles) and internally (values, attitudes, and beliefs).

The Anglo conformity (Cole & Cole, 1954) view of acculturation has historically mingled with a variety of ethnocentric views, but its central assumption rests on the desirability of maintaining English institutions (as modified by American history), the English language, and selected English cultural patterns. Thus, this view is exclusive in that acculturation is viewed as desirable only if the Anglo–Saxon cultural pattern is taken as the ideal. By implication, all other cultural forms are of less value, status, and importance. At present, the American quest for a unique national character is following the path marked by the Anglo conformity view of America as a melting pot.

The Anglo conformity view of acculturation reached its peak of intensity during the Americanization movement which swept the United States during World War I and extended into the 1920s and 1930s. One writer (Gordon, 1964) characterized this movement as a draconian attempt at "pressure-cooker assimilation," stripping the immigrant of his native culture and attachments and making him into an American along the Anglo–Saxon image. Public education, an institution controlling the social destiny of the individual, not only developed a negative view of the children of the immigrant but also formulated a set of goals for these children. For example, having described the new southern and eastern European as "illiterate," "docile," "lacking in self-reliance, initiative," etc., a noted educator of that day, E. P. Cubberley (1909), vividly stated appropriate goals of American public education for both the immigrant parent and his children:

> . . . everywhere these people settle in groups or settlements, and . . . set up their national manners, customs, and observances. Our task is to break up these groups or settlements, to assimilate and amalgamate these people as part of our American race, and to implant in their children, as far as can be done, the Anglo–Saxon conception of righ-

teousness, law and order, and our popular government, and to awaken in them a reverence for our democratic institutions and for those things in our national life which we as a people hold to be of abiding worth [pp. 15–16].

Cubberley's remarks may seem exceedingly harsh, but despite his phraseology, the underlying assumptions are clearly present in today's efforts to rationalize the relatively low achievement of many Mexican American children and of current efforts at compensatory education.

It is clear from both versions of the melting pot that the cultural values, beliefs, and customs of nonacculturated groups are viewed as varying in value, status, and importance. Thus the values, beliefs, and customs are not considered comparable to those characteristics of the American middle class. If they are not comparable, then they are assumed to be deficient, and are thought to produce lower socioeconomic conditions. In the case of Mexican Americans, they themselves and their culture and its values are considered the ultimate and final cause of their low socioeconomic status (Heller, 1971). This assumption, which we shall term the "damaging-culture" assumption, has been particularly prominent both in the rationalizing of the low academic achievement of Mexican American children and as a basis for educational policy and practice. The "damaging-culture" assumption as it has been applied to Mexican Americans has consistently led to the conclusion that the culture of Mexican Americans socializes individuals to become lazy, resigned, passive, fatalistic, nongoal-oriented, docile, shy, infantile, criminally prone, irrational, emotional, authoritarian, unreliable, limited in cognitive ability, untrustworthy, lax, priest-ridden, and nonachievement-oriented.

Despite aspirations to objectivity, the damaging-culture assumption has been pervasive in social science studies of Mexican Americans, and variants of this assumption can be found in sociology (Bryan, 1912; Humphrey, 1944; Landes, 1965; Tuck, 1946; Walker, 1928), in psychology (Garretson, 1928; Griffith, 1948; Haught, 1931; Young, 1922), and in anthropology (Clark, 1959; Edmonson, 1957; Kluckhohn & Strodtbeck, 1961; Rubel, 1966). Such studies have contributed to the view of Mexican American children as *products of a culture dominated by values that make learning difficult.*

The Theory of Compensatory Education

A series of papers described the theoretical and research basis for the notion that preschool programs for children from low-income families can compensate for environmental, cultural, and social deprivation (C. Deutsch, 1964; M. Deutsch 1964; Hunt, 1964; John & Goldstein, 1964; Whiteman, 1964). The theory of intervention or compensatory education, as usually stated in the 1960s, reasoned that a large number of children from impoverished homes were failing in school because they were growing up in a "disadvantaged" or "deprived" environment that did not provide the stimuli necessary for success in school. This reasoning led to the notion that it is necessary to intervene in the environment and provide compensatory education before these children enter school and during their early school years. The rationale for this approach was grounded in research with animals and humans which demonstrated that under highly unusual environmental circumstances physical and mental development can be retarded. What is often ignored in these studies is the fact that these environmental circumstances are *highly* unusual and bear serious questioning before any educational policy should evolve from them. The research has shown that monkeys who are almost completely deprived of sensory or social experiences, or dogs raised in complete isolation, or a child kept in an attic with little care or attention for the first 6 years of her life, or infants raised in an unstimulating institutional environment for orphans do show mental, physical, and emotional retardation. These findings in themselves are not necessarily startling. What is startling, however, is that the stark imagery of isolation, complete laboratory restriction of sensory and social stimulation, or imprisonment in an attic for the first 6 years of life became translated into the imagery of the typical environment for all low-income children, an image that supported the damaging-culture assumption.

Carter (1970) has pointed out that the theory underlying compensatory education, the theory of cultural deprivation, implies that certain nurturing cultures do not provide the necessary influence to make children successful in school or acceptable in the major society. Furthermore, it is implied that the principal role of the school is to act as the first of a chain of influences that will cause "disadvantaged" children to accept middle-class culture. It is the school's function in society to reeducate these children. Also implicit is the assumption that the school is essentially satisfactory as it now exists and that it is a valid representation of American culture. Thus the theories underlying compensatory education and the two variants of the melting-pot theory clearly and mutually reinforce the conception of each that something about the child is wrong and that the schools represent the cultural standards to which all must conform.

Mexican Americans, Modernization, and the Ideology of Universalism

Within the context of an image of the United States as a modern, industrialized nation with a highly sophisticated and complex level of technology, the Mexican American population is often viewed as a monolithic and static "folk" culture, emphasizing the "quaint" and "romantic." Fein (1970) has recently pointed out that one aspect of the ideology of modernization has been its commitment, in education as in other spheres, to the belief that modern industrial society requires a transformation of "folk" culture. This precept underlies many of the social sciences, especially those concerned with modernizations. According to this view, the passage from "traditional" to "modern" society involves complex changes in the organization of the society. There is presumed to be a movement from identification with primary groups to identification with secondary groups, from social norms in which status is derived from a place in the social order to the derivation of status from the function that one performs in society and how well one performs it (achievement). It is a movement toward more complex, highly differentiated, and specialized social institutions and social roles. In modern complex societies, the four basic structures (kinship, territorial community, social stratification, and ethnic groupings) are interlaced and overlaid by economic and political systems that are organized in a considerable part on radically different principles—the principles of achieved, competitive placement rather than ascription by birth, of impersonal *universalistic* norms, and of narrowly defined relations among persons. The stress of the ideology of modernization is on *universalism, secularism,* and *rationality* as against *traditionalism, ritualism,* and *community.*

This commitment to *universalism* reinforces the ideology of the melting pot with its own commitment to the nationalizing, standardizing, and homogenizing of cultural diversity. The fate of cultural diversity from the perspective of the ideology of universalism is readily inferred from the remarks of Shibutani and Kwan (1965):

> The basic differences between ethnic groups are cultural, and conventional norms serve as masks to cover the similarities. Whenever men interact informally, the common human nature comes through. It would appear, then, that it is only a matter of time before a more enlightened citizenry will realize this. Then, there will be a realignment of group loyalties, and ethnic identity will become a thing of the past [p. 589].

The ideology of universalism has pervaded efforts to understand the dynamics of modernization despite decades (even centuries) of evidence of the persistence of adherence to community, regional, and ethnic loyalties—an area of study that has occupied the attention and interest of scholars such as Nisbet (1962) and Glazer and Moynihan (1963). The ideology of universalism poses serious problems even for the American middle-class perspective. McDavid (1969) comments:

> We need to tease apart the various elements of middle-class socialization and determine which values, beliefs, or habits are *universally* serviceable ones, as opposed to others which are trivial and superficial. . . . To resolve this question about the *validity* of middle-class values which are the backbone of public school socialization, we need to break down the stereotype into its components, and to ascertain which (if any) elements may be *serviceable universally* for all members of our society, which may be of limited service to members of some subcultures but not others, and which (if any) may simply be useless and superfluous residues of *traditionalism* [pp. 6–7; emphasis added].

It is often within the context of both the melting-pot ideology and the ideology of universalism that the values, beliefs, and socialization practices of Mexican Americans are criticized, with the conclusion that the culture prevents achievement in a modern society, that such residues of traditionalism hamper mobility and academic success.

Mexican Americans:
Homogeneity versus Heterogeneity

One of the major obstacles preventing the formulation of a coherent educational policy for Mexican Americans is the persistent notion that the Mexican American population constitutes a homogeneous group. It is true that the Mexican American population has been characterized by a pervasive low economic status and low academic achievement. This had led at least one sociologist (Heller, 1966) to characterize the Mexican American population as marked by a "lack of internal differentiation and therefore constituting an unusually homogeneous ethnic group." Unfortunately, the concentration on such variables as economic status and educational achievement has almost successfully obscured the highly diverse and heterogeneous character of the Mexican American population in many other important spheres of life. Social scientists have neglected to describe the diversity of child-socialization practices in the Mexican American population and the effects of these practices on personality development and behavior. Such information is crucial for any attempt to develop educational policy or plan educational programs.

Although we use the term *Mexican American,* we recognize that it is not acceptable to some sectors of this population group—for example, Spanish Americans of northern New Mexico and southern Colorado. Indeed, the diversity of Mexican Americans is implied in the variety of names designating the population, e.g., Spanish Americans, Latin Americans, Chicanos, Hispanos, Spanish-speaking, and La Raza.

The historical, genetic, and cultural heterogeneity of Mexican Americans is a varied and highly complex affair. For example, the Spanish and Indian components may range from 100 to 0%. Furthermore, the Spanish component in itself is highly heterogeneous. The Spaniard was, and is, a complex of original Iberian man, Greek, Latin, Visigoth, Moroccan, Phoenician, Carthaginian, and others. The degree to which a Spaniard was, or is, more of one or of some small combination of these varies in the Catalans, the Gallegos, and the Basques, etc., as evidenced by wide differences in physical features and languages. The Indian component is no less complex. There were, and still are, numerous major Indian groups—the early Spaniards called them "nations" because they had such distinctly different physical, social, economic, and cultural characteristics. The Mayas of southeastern Mexico are far removed culturally, and in many other ways from the Yaquis of northwestern Mexico, and from the Tarahumaras, the Otomis, the Miztecs, and the Zapotecs, etc. And all of them are equally removed from one another. Add to this the fact that the Spaniards trickled into New Spain over a period of 300 years and settled in regions that for the most part were isolated from one another.

Despite the diversity in background of the Mexican American population, the general public image that has persisted is that of older, agricultural workers. In fact, approximately 80% of the population lives and works in urban areas and it is one of the youngest of America's population groups.

The Damaging-Culture View of Mexican Americans

The theory that the culture and values of Mexican Americans are the ultimate and final cause of their low economic status and low academic achievement—the damaging-culture view—has been almost exclusively the framework within which social scientists have written about Mexican Americans (Clark, 1959; Edmonson, 1957; Garretson, 1928; Garth, 1923; Haught, 1931; Humphrey, 1944; Kluckhohn & Strodtbeck, 1961; Landes, 1965; Rubel, 1966; Saunders, 1954; Tuck, 1946; Walker, 1928; Young, 1922). Perhaps the person who has written most extensively from the damaging-culture point of view has been Heller (1966, 1971). Her work has been selected for more comment since the focus of her conclusions has been on the socialization practices of the Mexican American home.

Heller has attempted to discover why Mexican Americans constitute the only major ethnic group with no substantial intergenerational rise in socioeconomic status. Her work is based on questionnaire data acquired in 1955 and interview data obtained approximately

10 years later. Females were not represented in the study (high school students). Her conclusions have pointed implications from the damaging-culture view for Mexican American socialization in the areas of *communication, human relations, motivation,* and *learning.* According to Heller, Mexican Americans have a language problem with a foreign accent often persisting to the third generation, are trained for dependent behavior, seldom show initiative or freely express their own ideas, and do not provide the kind of independent training that is highly functional for achievement. Their progress, Heller has said, is retarded by large families, they manifest an unusual persistence in traditional forms, and children are not socialized in the habits of self-discipline necessary to satisfactory school performance. Many other such generalizations implying that Mexican American children are products of a culture dominated by values that make it difficult for them to learn in the American public schools can be found in Heller's work.

As we have attempted to show in this chapter, the damaging-culture view of Mexican Americans finds its ideological origins in the theory of the melting pot, the ideology of modernization, and stereotyping based on a view of Mexican Americans as a homogeneous population, all of which have currently combined with the theory of cultural deprivation underlying the concept of compensatory education.

Adjustment and Identity

Educational policies based on the melting pot can produce conflict in Mexican American students which leads to two different modes of personal adjustment. For example, Ramírez (1970) found that Mexican American junior high and high school students who identified exclusively with Anglo–American values described themselves as having many disagreements with their parents but having pleasant relationships outside the home. The following is a statement characteristic of a student in this group:

> I don't want to be known as a Mexican American, but only as American. I was born in this country and raised among Americans. I think like an

Anglo, I talk like one, and I dress like one. It's true I don't look like an Anglo and sometimes I am rejected by them, but it would be worse if I spoke Spanish or said that I was of Mexican descent. I am sorry I do not get along well with my parents, but their views are old fashioned. They still see themselves as Mexican, and they do not understand me. Often we have arguments, but I ignore them. In fact, I had to move away from my home because of our disagreements. I wish those people who are always making noise about being Mexican Americans would be quiet. We would all be better off if they would accept things as they are. I just want a good education. I don't want to be poor or discriminated against [p. 120].

Another group of Mexican American students identified themselves exclusively with traditional Mexican American values and described themselves as having pleasant and satisfying relationships with their parents; they were well adjusted at home but felt alienated from people outside of the home. The following statement is characteristic of students in this group (Ramírez, 1970):

I am proud of being a Mexican American. We have a rich heritage. Mexico is a great country that is progressing fast. It has a wonderful history and culture. My family is the most important thing in the world for me. I owe my parents everything and I will never complain when they need me. I don't want to be like the Anglos because they don't care about their families; they just care about themselves and making money. They don't like anybody who is different. At school, the teachers ignored you if they knew you weren't going to college, and most of us Mexicans couldn't afford to go. The things I learned at school were against what my parents had taught me. I had to choose my parents, because they are old and they need my help and understanding. Most people, even some Mexican Americans look down on us because we are Mexicans, and I hate them. It is unhealthy and unnatural to want to be something you are not [p. 121].

The effect of the melting-pot philosophy, then, is to encourage a one-sided identity among Mexican American students, to force them to choose to identify with either the culture of the home or that of the school. The educational policies based on the melting pot do not provide the opportunity for a third option—the opportunity to develop a bicultural identity which permits the child to enjoy satisfying relations in more than one cultural world and to identify with aspects of both of those cultures.

One of our ultimate interests is to help Mexican Americans develop a bicultural identity such as that reflected in the following statements (Ramírez, 1970):

> I am happy to be an American of Mexican descent. Because I am a Mexican I learned to be close to my family, and they have been a source of strength and support for me. If things ever got too bad on the outside I could always come to them for comfort and understanding. My Spanish also helped me a lot in my education and will also open a lot of doors for me when I look for a job. As an American I am happy to live in a great progressive country where we have the freedom to achieve anything we want. I feel all I have achieved I owe to the help of my parents, the encouragement of my teachers, and the chance to live in this country. I feel very rich and fortunate because I have two cultures rather than just one [p. 121].

Summary

The Anglo conformity view of the melting pot considers acculturation as desirable only if the Anglo–American middle-class cultural pattern is taken as ideal. By implication, all other cultural forms are considered to be of less value, status, and importance. "Compensatory" education in the United States has operated under the assumption that Mexican American culture and the Spanish language interfere with the intellectual and emotional development of children. These educational practices, then, encourage Mexican American children to reject their identity with Mexican American culture and to accept the value system of the mainstream American middle class. This produces conflict in Mexican American students and leads them to conclude that they cannot identify with two cultures but must reject either Mexican American or mainstream American middle-class culture. An educational philosophy which encourages policies and practices aimed toward developing a bicultural identity in Mexican American children must be formulated. Such a philosophy is discussed in the next chapter.

References

Bryan, S. Mexican immigrants in the United States. *The Survey*, 1912, **28**, 726–730.

Carter, T. P. *Mexican Americans in school: A history of educational neglect.* New York: College Entrance Examination Board, 1970.

Clark, M. *Health in the Mexican American culture: A community study.* Berkeley, California: University of California Press, 1959.

Cole, S. G., & Cole, M. W. *Minorities and the American Promise.* New York: Harper, 1954.

Crevecoeur, J. H. St. J. (Michael-Guillaume St. John de Crevecoeur). *Letters from an American farmer.* New York: Fox, Duffield & Co., 1904.

Cubberley, E. P. *Changing conceptions of education.* Boston, Massachusetts: Houghton, 1909.

Deutsch, C. P. Auditory discrimination and learning social factors. *Merrill-Palmer Quarterly of Behavior and Development,* 1964, **10**:3, 277–296.

Deutsch, M. Facilitating development in the pre-school child: Social and psychological perspectives. *Merrill-Palmer Quarterly of Behavior and Development,* 1964, **10**:3, 249–264.

Dewey, J. Nationalizing education. National Education Association of the United States, *Addresses and Proceedings of the Fifty-fourth Annual Meeting,* 1916. Pp. 185–186. Cited by M. M. Gordon, *Assimilation in American life: The role of race, religion and national origins.* London and New York: Oxford Univ. Press, 1964. Pp. 139–140.

Edmonson, S. *Los Manitos: A study of institutional values.* New Orleans: Middle American Research Institute, Tulane University, 1957.

Fein, L. J. Community schools and social theory: The limits of universalism. In H. M. Levin (Ed.), *Community control of schools.* New York: Simon & Shuster, 1970.

Garretson, O. K. A study of retardation among Mexican children in a small public school system in Arizona. *Journal of Educational Psychology,* 1928, **19**, 31–40.

Garth, T. R. A comparison of the intelligence of Mexican and mixed and full blood Indian children. *Psychological Review,* 1923, **30**, 388–401.

Glazer, N., & Moynihan, D. P. *Beyond the melting pot: The Negroes, Puerto Ricans, Jews, Italians, and Irish of New York City.* (2nd ed.) Cambridge, Massachusetts: MIT Press, 1963.

Gordon, M. M. *Assimilation in American life: The role of race, religion and national origins.* London and New York: Oxford Univ. Press, 1964.

Griffith, B. W. *American me.* Boston, Massachusetts: Houghton, 1948.

Hansen, M. L. *The immigrant in American history.* Cambridge, Massachusetts: Harvard Univ. Press, 1948.

Haught, B. F. The language difficulty of Spanish-American children. *Journal of Applied Psychology,* 1931, **15,** 92–95.

Heller, C. *Mexican American youth: Forgotten youth at the crossroads.* New York: Random House, 1966.

Heller, C. *New converts to the American dream?* New Haven, Connecticut: College & University Press, 1971.

Humphrey, N. D. The changing structure of the Detroit Mexican family. *American Sociological Review,* 1944, **9**(6), 622–626.

Hunt, J. Mc V. The psychological bases for using pre-school enrichment as an antidote for cultural deprivation. *Merrill-Palmer Quarterly of Behavior and Development,* 1964, **10**:3, 209–248.

John, V. P., & Goldstein, L. S. The social context of language acquisition. *Merrill-Palmer Quarterly of Behavior and Development,* 1964, **10**:3, 265–276.

Kluckhohn, F., & Strodtbeck, F. L. *Variations in value orientations.* New York: Harper, 1961.

Landes, R. *Latin Americans of the Southwest.* St. Louis, Missouri: Webster Division, McGraw-Hill, 1965.

McDavid, J. The teacher as an agent of socialization. In E. Grotberg (Ed.), *Critical issues in research related to disadvantaged children.* Princeton, New Jersey: Educational Testing Service, 1969.

Moore, J., & Cuellar, A. *Mexican Americans.* Englewood Cliffs, New Jersey: Prentice-Hall, 1970.

Nisbet, R. A. *Community and power.* London and New York: Oxford Univ. Press, 1962. Originally published: *The quest for community,* 1953.

Ramírez III, M. Identity crisis in Mexican American adolescents. In H. S. Johnson, & M. W. Hernandez (Eds.), *Educating the Mexican American.* Valley Forge, Pennsylvania: Judson Press, 1970.

Rubel, A. J. *Across the tracks: Mexican Americans in a Texas city.* Austin, Texas: Hogg Foundation for Mental Health, University of Texas Press, 1966.

Saunders, L. *Cultural difference and medical care: The case of the Spanish-speaking people of the Southwest.* New York: Russell Sage Foundation, 1954.

Shibutani, T., & Kwan, K. M. *Ethnic stratification: A comparative approach.* New York: MacMillan 1965.

Tuck, R. *Not with the fist: Mexican Americans in a southwest city.* New York: Harcourt, 1946.

United States Commission on Civil Rights: Mexican American Education Study. Reports I–V. 1971–1973. U.S. GPO, Washington, D. C.

Report I: Ethnic isolation of Mexican Americans in the public schools of the Southwest. 1971a.

Report II: The unfinished education: Outcomes for minorities in the five southwestern states. 1971b.

Report III: The excluded student; educational practices affecting Mexican Americans in the Southwest. 1972a.

Report IV: Mexican American education in Texas; a function of wealth. 1972b.

Report V: Teacher and students; differences in teacher interaction with Mexican American and Anglo students. 1973.

Walker, H. Mexican immigrants as laborers. *Sociology and Social Research,* 1928, **13,** 55–62.

Whiteman, M. Intelligence and learning. *Merrill-Palmer Quarterly of Behavior and Development,* 1964, **10**:3, 297–309.

Young, K. *Mental differences in certain immigrant groups.* Eugene, Oregon: University of Oregon Publications, **1**(11), 1922.

2

Cultural Democracy
in Education

Introduction

The American ideology of assimilation embodied in the theory of the melting pot as a basis for educational policy is vividly illustrated by the following reproduction reflecting the "No Spanish Rule" adopted by many districts in the Southwest until very recently.

VIOLATION SLIP—SPANISH DETENTION

_____ was speaking
(Student's name and classification)
Spanish during school hours. This pupil must report to Spanish Detention in the Cafeteria on the assigned day. (The teacher reporting should place the date on this slip.)

_____   _____
(Dates to report)   (Teacher reporting)
Return this slip to Mr. _____ or Mr. _____
before 3:30 p.m. 9/66

As reported by the United States Civil Rights Commission (1972), the violation slip reproduced (p. 21) was used to place children in "Spanish Detention Class" in a school district in Texas. Although the survey reported in this Civil Rights Commission Report did not uncover instances in which school officials admitted to administering physical punishment for speaking Spanish, allegations concerning such punishment were heard by the Commission at its hearing in San Antonio (1968). Moreover, other forms of punishment are revealed in the following excerpts from the themes of one class of seventh-grade Mexican American students in Texas. They were written as part of an assignment to describe their elementary school experiences and their teachers' attitudes toward speaking Spanish in school.

If we spoke Spanish we had to pay 5¢ to the teacher or we had to stay after school.

In the first through the fourth grade, if the teacher caught us talking Spanish we would have to stand on the "black square" for an hour or so.

When I was in elementary they had a rule not to speak Spanish but we all did. If you got caught speaking Spanish you were to write three pages saying, "I must not speak Spanish in school."

In the sixth grade, they kept a record of which if we spoke Spanish they would take it down and charge us a penny for every Spanish word. If we spoke more than one thousand words our parents would have to come to school and talk with the principal.

If you'd been caught speaking Spanish you would be sent to the principal's office or given extra assignments to do as homework or probably made to stand by the wall during recess and after school [U.S. Commission on Civil Rights: Mexican American Study Report III: *The Excluded Student,* May 1972, pp. 18, 19].

In this same report, an interview with a school principal revealed that he would "fight teaching Spanish past the third grade because it destroys loyalty to America [p. 20]." This assertion, in our opinion, reflects an unfounded fear, a fear that reinforces the ideology of the Anglo conformity view of acculturation. This fear may explain in part why American public education struggles to keep alive the principles of political and economic democracy, and yet has ranged from ambivalence to open antagonism toward the child's struggle

to remain identified with his or her own home and community socialization experiences.

It is to this issue that the Office of Civil Rights, Department of
Health, Education and Welfare, attempts to speak via posters which
contain faces of Mexican American children with the following
inscriptions:

Yo tengo derecho a mi idioma y mi cultura.
I have a right to my language and my culture.

Saber me idioma y mi cultura me ayuda a ser un buen ciudadano.
Knowing my language and my culture will help me to become a good
    citizen.

El Acta de los Derechos Civiles de 1964 protege mis derechos de poder
    hablar mi idioma y de continuar mi cultura.
The Civil Rights Act of 1964 protects my right to speak my language
    and continue to identify with my culture.

Cultural Democracy

The implications of the Civil Rights posters refer to the legal rights
of an individual to be different while at the same time being a responsible member of a larger society. More specifically, cultural
democracy, as we define it, states that an individual can be bicultural and still be loyal to American ideals. Cultural democracy is
a philosophical precept which recognizes that the way a person
communicates, relates to others, seeks support and recognition from
his environment (incentive motivation), and thinks and learns (cognition) is a product of the value system of his home and community.
Furthermore, educational environments or policies that do not recognize the individual's right, as guaranteed by the Civil Rights Act of
1964, to remain identified with the culture and language of his cultural group are culturally undemocratic.

Biculturalism and American Public Education

Whatever its intention, any educational policy (such as those
based on the Anglo conformity view of acculturation) that keeps a

Mexican American child from learning or valuing Spanish or Mexican American cultural values creates painful psychological problems for the child. The school's rejection of the Spanish language or of anything in his life which is related to Mexican American culture implies rejection of the child himself. Instead of providing the opportunity to establish a bicultural identity, such policies force the child to make a choice of identifying with one culture rather than the other. Most difficult of all, such policies exert pressure on the child to make a choice at a time in his life when the values that he has acquired at home are not consciously articulable by the child. Consequently, one of the basic principles of democracy, that of conscious choice, is being violated by such policies.

The philosophy of cultural democracy requires that the school refrain from making the choice for the child. A culturally democratic learning environment is a setting in which a Mexican American child can acquire knowledge about his own culture and the dominant culture; the learning, furthermore, is based on communication, human–relational, incentive–motivational, and learning patterns that are culturally appropriate. The goal of such an environment is to develop biculturalism with regard to communication, human relations, motivation, and learning. The educational goal is to help children learn to function competently and effectively in, as well as to contribute to, more than one cultural world.

Cultural Pluralism and Cultural Democracy

Historical Origins

The concept of cultural democracy has its roots in an alternative ideology that emerged in reaction to the Anglo conformity view of acculturation. The threat to cultural diversity posed by this conformity view spurred the development of a new line of thought designed to promote cultural diversity in the United States: Under the general term "cultural pluralism," ideas designed to counteract or moderate the impact of the Anglo conformity view of acculturation became part of the national dialog shortly after the turn of the century.

In a two-part essay entitled *Democracy versus the Melting Pot,* Kallen (1915) rejected the melting-pot theories and the Anglo conformity views of acculturation as models of what was actually transpiring in American life. Observing a vigorously continuing ethnic existence in many different parts of the United States, Kallen felt that America stood at a kind of cultural crossroads. America could persist in policies implied by the melting pot or encourage its ethnic groups to develop democratically by way of each emphasizing its own deep-rooted culture. Kallen (1924) argued for the possibility of a democratic commonwealth as implied in the following:

> Its form would be that of the federal republic; its substance a democracy of nationalities, cooperating voluntarily and autonomously through common institutions in the enterprise of self-realization through the perfection of men according to their kind. The common language . . . of its great tradition, would be English, but each nationality would have for its emotional involuntary life its own peculiar dialect or speech, its own individual and inevitable esthetic and intellectual forms. The political and economic life of the commonwealth is a single unit and serves as the foundation and background for the realization of the distinctive individuality of each *natio* that composes it and of the pooling of these in a harmony above them all [p. 124].

Kallen (1915) fundamentally believed that:

> . . . the United States are in the process of becoming a federal state not merely as a union of geographical and administrative unities, but also as a cooperation of cultural diversities, as a federation or commonwealth of national cultures [p. 116].

Kallen proposed this to be the more or less inevitable consequence of democratic ideals since individuals constitute groups, and democracy for the individual must, by implication, also mean democracy for the group. Thus, Kallen interpreted the term "equal" as it appears in the Declaration of Independence, and the Preamble and the Amendments to the Constitution, as affirmation of the right to be different. While Kallen's writings, in which he coined the term "cultural pluralism," have many aspects, his theme of a "federation of nationalities," with its implication for the creation of geoethnic states, as well as the suggestion that the individual's fate is predetermined by his ethnic group membership, caused some distress among the ranks of the other cultural pluralists.

Cultural Pluralism and the Democratic Idea of Choice

Kallen's emphasis on the individual's right to retain his ethnic identity brought about considerable discussion among other cultural pluralists who were concerned with the democratic theme or principle of freedom of choice. Specifically, Berkson (1920) and Drachsler (1920) adopted the position that different ethnic groups should have the right to maintain an ethnic identity and even proposed a variety of ways this might be done, e.g., the creation of ethnic communal centers, or after-public-school-hour ethnic schools. They both favored efforts by the ethnic community to maintain its communal and cultural life, providing a rich and flavorful environment for its successive generations, and they felt that the government should institute in the public schools a program emphasizing knowledge and appreciation of the various cultures. Drachsler argued, however, that whether or not some groups continued to maintain their separate communal existence would be a course legitimately sanctioned by democratic values, since the choice of whether to fuse or to remain separate, either for the group or the individual, should be a free one. This choice, which Drachsler felt should be added to the older American ideas of political and economic democracy, he labeled "cultural democracy."

At the abstract, philosophical level, in both Drachsler's and Berkson's ideas, an important question arose: Cultural pluralism may be democratic for groups, but how democratic is it for individuals? The choice of whether or not to "melt" should be a free one. In his more recent book, *Assimilation in American Life,* Gordon (1964) summarizes this issue:

> The system of cultural pluralism . . . has frequently been described as "cultural democracy," since it posits the right of ethnic groups in a democratic society to maintain their communal identity and their own subcultural values. . . . however, we must also point out that democratic values prescribe free choice not only for groups but also for individuals. That is, the individual, *as he matures and reaches the age where rational decision* is feasible, should be allowed to choose freely

whether to remain within the boundaries of communality created by his birthright ethnic group, to branch out into multiple interethnic contacts, or even to change affiliation to that of another ethnic group should he wish to do so . . . . If, to the contrary, the ethnic group places such heavy pressures on its birthright members to stay confined to ethnic communality that the individual who consciously wishes to "branch out" or "move away" feels intimidated or subject to major feelings of personal guilt and therefore remains ethnically enclosed, or moves but at a considerable psychological cost, then we have, in effect, cultural democracy for groups but not for individuals. Realistically, *it is probably impossible to have a socialization process for the child growing up in a particular ethnic group that does not involve some implicitly restrictive values; nevertheless, the magnitude and intensity of such restrictive norms must be kept within bounds if we are not to be left with a system which provides cultural democracy for groups but enforced ethnic enclosure for individuals* [pp. 262–263; emphasis added].

Biculturalism and the Concept of Choice

Gordon's analysis contains, from our own perspective, the dilemma of choice which has permeated most views on cultural pluralism. This dilemma is in part due to a persisting view of personality development which contains *mono-* rather than *bi-* or *multi-*cultural orientations. Thus, Gordon's (1964) statement appears to be more concerned with the abstract philosophical democratic principle of "freedom of choice."

> . . . the individual, as he matures and reaches the age where rational decision is feasible, should be allowed to choose freely whether to remain within the boundaries of communality created by his birthright ethnic group, to branch out into multiple interethnic contacts, or even to change affiliation to that of another ethnic group should he wish to do so [p. 263].

We note, however, that Gordon's analysis, with the term "branch out into multiple interethnic contacts," appears to restrict or exclude other potential options involved in choice as it relates to cultural matters. As with other interpretations of cultural democracy, it appears to us that Gordon's interpretation raises the issue of choice as being of the either/or category: The individual either chooses to remain ethnic or chooses to acculturate. This interpretation of cultural democracy appears to assume an *unresolvable conflict or incompatibility* between the "dominant" sociocultural system and other sociocultural systems.

The form of cultural pluralism we wish to describe more fully concentrates on the *bicultural* reality of many Mexican American children living in the United States today. On the one hand, at the time these children enter school, they are products of the sociocultural system characteristic of their homes and communities. They are now confronted, on the other hand, with being required to acquire the characteristics inherent in the sociocultural system of the school which, we have indicated, is more compatible with the Anglo–American sociocultural systems. The basic educational issue in our interpretation of cultural democracy concerns the need for providing Mexican American children with the educational experiences necessary to enhance their right to be able to function in *both* cultural worlds, the cultural world of the Mexican American as well as the cultural world of the Anglo–American. In one sense *both* the Anglo conformity views of acculturation and older interpretations of cultural pluralism have failed to appreciate this psychological necessity on the part of the child. Within the melting-pot framework, Mexican American children have been forced to make the type of choice implied in Gordon's statement and at times in their lives when the ability to make such a "rational choice" has been least developed and the psychological costs of making such a choice considerable.

The writings of many cultural pluralists have placed a major emphasis on the preservation of the language, heritage, and cultural values of the ethnic group. Perhaps this concern has been historically necessary in that the Anglo conformity view of acculturation has been inimical to any notion implying preservation of cultural differences. The basic theme in our interpretation of cultural pluralism is not this preservation as such, but the ability to function in both cultural worlds, whatever their characteristics at any given point in time. The cultural worlds of both the Mexican American and the Anglo–American have undergone and are undergoing modification and change, and from an educational point of view it is important for the individual to be able to function in whichever cultural world he finds himself and at the same time to contribute to its enrichment and continued development.

The Bicultural Character of the World of
Mexican American Children: Educational Implications

If a Mexican American child has been raised during his preschool years in the sociocultural system characteristic of the traditional Mexican American community, the socialization practices pertaining to (1) language and heritage, (2) cultural values, and (3) teaching styles will be unique to that system, and the child will have developed a communication, learning, and motivational style which is appropriate to it. At the time the child begins his experience in the public schools he is required to relate to a sociocultural system whose socialization practices pertaining to language and heritage, cultural values, and teaching styles are different from those he experienced during his preschool years. In effect, it is a new cultural world which he must come to explore and understand. *At the same time* he must continue to explore, understand, and learn to function in the heretofore familiar sociocultural system, i.e., continue to develop the communication, learning, and motivational styles that are represented in his home and community. These demands placed on many Mexican American children in one sense constitute the reality of a bicultural world. The realities are in fact that the Mexican American child must (a) learn to function effectively in the mainstream American cultural community, and (b) continue to function effectively in and contribute to the Mexican American cultural community. The Anglo conformity view of acculturation in education has accepted only one of these realities: to function effectively and contribute to the mainstream American cultural world. This concept has excluded or prohibited from consideration the child's need to function effectively in and contribute to the Mexican American cultural world. The concept of cultural democracy which we propose is based on this bicultural reality of the Mexican American child's world and has as its primary educational goal, *the ability to function effectively in and the responsibility to contribute to developments in both cultural worlds.* Under this concept of cultural democracy in education, the term "equal educational opportunity" can be interpreted to mean that the school is obligated to create programs of such a nature that the child acquires the skills that are necessary to his functioning in and contributing to both worlds. This perspective for education assumes bicultural educational methodologies: The child is permitted to explore new sociocultural systems within the framework of the "cultural forms and loyalties" (Baratz & Baratz, 1970) that constitute his home and community sociocultural system. In terms of social and intellectual development, then, the educational goal of a bicultural educational program is a *bicultural identity.* This is the fundamental underlying assumption of a program in bicultural education within the framework of cultural democracy.

Although, in reality, the American Southwest is historically and culturally a multicultural entity, many non-Mexican American children are denied the opportunity to freely explore Mexican American language and heritage, cultural values, and teaching styles—a denial that is one of the direct results of the Anglo conformity view of acculturation in education. As a consequence, many non-Mexican American children living in the American Southwest have been denied the opportunity to function effectively in or contribute to developments in the Mexican American cultural world. Thus, many of these children who will become doctors, lawyers, teachers, etc., will be unable to function effectively in their professional roles when working with Mexican American populations.

A Bicultural Perspective for Implementing Culturally Democratic Educational Environments

In Table 2.1 we have summarized and schematically highlighted the principal differences between melting-pot and culturally democratic views of the Mexican American sociocultural system, indicating where the emphasis on change is placed, as well as the ultimate educational goals of each.

As can be inferred from Table 2.1, the educational task becomes one of minimizing the "restrictive values" that, according to Gordon (1964), lead to a system which "provides cultural democracy for groups but enforced ethnic enclosure for individuals [p. 263]." Our view, however, is that these "restrictive values" have resided in the educational policies and practices of the Anglo conformity view of

TABLE 2.1

Differences between the Exclusivist Melting-Pot and the Culturally Democratic Philosophies in Education

Philosophy	Mexican American sociocultural system	Socialization practices of Mexican American home and community	Personality characteristics	What is changed	Goal
Melting pot—Anglo conformity view	Excluded, omitted, prohibited, or considered educationally unimportant	Seen as interfering with child's development. The basis of deprivation	Seen as deviant, unacceptable, "culturally deprived"	The child	Acculturation into the cultural ideal of Anglo-American middle class
Cultural democracy	Language–heritage, cultural values, and teaching styles considered educationally important	Seen as determining unique communication, human–relational, incentive–motivational, and cognitive styles and must be used as basis for teacher training	Seen as acceptable and as means whereby child can explore new cultural forms related to communication, human relations, incentive motivation, and cognition	The educational style of school through greater involvement of Mexican American parents, new teaching strategies, curriculum developments, and assessment techniques	Bicultural identity

acculturation that have prevented the development of bicultural orientations to education. Thus, the focus of change under a culturally democratic view of education is placed on the school, rather than on the child or his community. The reason for this lies in the assumption that the "restrictive values" that, according to Gordon, discourage interethnic relations, reside in *institutional* expressions of the Anglo conformity view of acculturation, rather than in an inherent socialization practice of any particular ethnic group. Where such "restrictive values" are observed in the case of any ethnic group, the strong possibility exists that these represent *adaptive* values in reaction to the exclusion or prohibition that the ethnic group may have experienced as the result of the Anglo conformity view of acculturation. This is in keeping with the observation that many ethnic groups in the United States have developed some variant of the thought, "one is less likely to be hurt by one's own kind."

From an educational perspective, one of the key assumptions is that the sociocultural system of the child's home and community is influential in producing culturally unique preferred modes of relating to others, especially authority figures; culturally unique incentive preferences, i.e., those environmental events which symbolize acceptance, recognition, and support; as well as a preferred mode of thinking, perceiving, remembering, and problem solving. All of these characteristics, under our conception of a culturally democratic educational environment, must be incorporated as the principal bases upon which programs for instituting changes in the school must be developed. The interest in their incorporation would not only be for their continued development but also as the medium through which the child is instructed in subject content and through which he explores other values, beliefs, incentive–motivational preferences, human–relational styles, and learning styles. In our conception a culturally democratic educational environment must pay critical attention to three important components: language and heritage, values, and teaching styles.

Language and Heritage

Literature concerning the language component is now substantial, and elsewhere (Cortés, 1971) guidelines for the treatment of Mexican

American history, historical figures, etc., have been developed. The involvement of Mexican American parents as contributors to the language and heritage components represents an immediate and critically important source for the schools. The writers of textbooks, editors, publishing companies, and school boards of education must be involved in the development of social studies material that is consistent with culturally democratic educational goals and practices.

Cultural Values

Although school programs might appear to have fewer administrative obstacles, at least in principle, in developing culturally democratic *language* and *heritage* components, the nature, form, and expression of differences in cultural *values* presents a more difficult problem for the schools. One failure has been a dismal lack on the part of teacher training to present the sociological, psychological, and anthropological characteristics of the different ethnic groups in this country. It is our opinion that such information must be presented from an educational perspective. Part of the failure is due to the very lack of such information; American social science has not been particularly oriented to the study of America's ethnic groups to any consistent degree or with any particular depth. In fact, another difficulty is that the sociological, anthropological, and psychological knowledge that does exist is influenced by the Anglo conformity view of acculturation with its concomitant deemphasis on the culturally diverse nature of American society. It is for such reasons that university campuses have experienced the rise and development of "ethnic studies."

Teaching Styles

One of the most critical consequences of the Anglo conformity view of acculturation has been to obscure understanding of different cultural value systems, as developed and expressed in the socialization practices of a given sociocultural system, and the manner in which these result in differences in learning styles. This possibility has emerged largely through the pioneering efforts of Bernstein (1961,

1962, 1964), Hess (1969), and Hess and Shipman (1965, 1967, 1968) who have developed the view that:

> . . . the child is socialized into modes of communication and strategies of thought that develop in response to specific interactions with salient adults, especially the mother. Adaptive consequences developed by the mother are transmitted through her linguistic modes, regulatory strategies, cognitive styles, and self-esteem. These early modes of dealing with the child induce similar adaptive consequences [Hess, 1969, pp. 40–41].

The work of Bernstein and Hess has concentrated on the modes, strategies, styles, etc. as they relate to membership in a particular socioeconomic class in England and the United States, respectively.

Table 2.2 depicts a critical concept: Ethnicity or differences in cultural values are as important as socioeconomic class—if not more so—in determination of the characteristics of the learning style of the child. Since the learning style is chiefly the result of the unique, culturally determined *teaching* styles, a culturally democratic

TABLE 2.2

Relationship of Ethnicity to Learning Style in Children

Ethnicity	Socialization practices of home and community (teaching styles)	Learning style of child	Areas of change for creating culturally democratic educational environments
Cultural values	Communication style	Preferred mode of communication	Communication
	Human–relational style	Preferred mode of relating	Human relations
	Incentive–motivational style	Incentive preference	Incentive motivation
	Cognition	Preferred mode of thinking, perceiving, remembering, and problem solving	Teaching style and curriculum

educational environment should incorporate the critical elements of the teaching styles characteristic of different cultural groups.

In order to reach the educational goals implied in Table 2.2, the three components, language and heritage, cultural values, and teaching styles must be fully implemented in American public education.

Summary

The philosophy of cultural democracy asserts that an individual can remain identified with the life style and values of his home and neighborhood while he becomes familiar with the life style and value system of the mainstream American middle class. Furthermore, it states that he should not be forced to make a decision before he fully understands the consequences of his choice. The concept of cultural democracy is based on the bicultural reality of the Mexican American child's world. The child must learn to function effectively in the mainstream American cultural world and also continue to function effectively in and contribute to the Mexican American cultural world.

From an educational perspective, one of the key assumptions is that the sociocultural system of the child's home and community is influential in producing unique preferred modes of communication, human relations, motivation, and learning. All of these characteristics must form the basis for developing culturally democratic educational environments that will ensure the success of Mexican American children in school. An initial step in developing culturally democratic educational environments is identifying the sociocultural system of Mexican Americans. The next chapter focuses on this value system.

References

Baratz, S. S., & Baratz, J. C. Early childhood intervention: The social science base of institutional racism. *Harvard Educational Review,* 1970, **40,** 29–50.

Berkson, I. B. *Theories of Americanization: A critical study with spe-*

cial reference to the Jewish group. New York: Teachers College, Columbia University, 1920.

Bernstein, B. Social class and linguistic development: A theory of social learning. In A. H. Halsey, J. Floud, & C. A. Anderson (Eds.), *Economy, education and society.* New York: Free Press of Glencoe, 1961.

Bernstein, B. Social class, linguistic codes and grammatical elements. *Language and Speech,* 1962, **5,** 31–46.

Bernstein, B. Elaborated and restricted codes: Their social origins and some consequences. *American Anthropologist,* 1964, **66** (6, pt. 2), 55–69.

Cortés, C. E. Revising the "All-American soul course": A bicultural avenue to educational reform. In A. Castañeda, M. Ramírez III, C. E. Cortés, & M. Barrera (Eds.), *Mexican Americans and educational change: Symposium at the University of California, Riverside, May 21–22, 1971.* New York: Arno, 1974.

Drachsler, J. *Democracy and assimilation: The blending of immigrant heritages in America.* New York: MacMillan, 1920.

Gordon, M. M. *Assimilation in American life: The role of race, religion, and national origins.* London and New York: Oxford Univ. Press, 1964.

Hess, R. D. Parental behavior and children's school achievement: Implications for Headstart. In E. Grotberg (Ed.), *Critical issues in research related to disadvantaged children.* Princeton, New Jersey: Educational Testing Service, 1969.

Hess, R. D., & Shipman, V. C. Early experience and the socialization of cognitive modes in children. *Child Development,* 1965, **36,** 869–886.

Hess, R. D., & Shipman, V. C. Cognitive elements in maternal behavior. In J. P. Hill (Ed.), *Minnesota symposia on child psychology,* Vol. 1. Minneapolis, Minnesota: Univ. of Minnesota Press, 1967.

Hess, R. D., & Shipman, V. C. Maternal attitudes toward the school and the role of pupil: Some social class comparisons. In A. H. Passow (Ed.), *Developing programs for the educationally disadvantaged.* New York: Teachers College, Columbia University, 1968.

Kallen, H. M. Democracy versus the melting pot. *The Nation,* Feb. 18 and 25, 1915. Reprinted in H. M. Kallen, *Culture and democracy in the United States.* New York: Boni and Liveright, 1924. P. 116.

Kallen, H. M. *Culture and democracy in the United States.* New York: Boni and Liveright, 1924.

United States Commission on Civil Rights: Hearing held in San Antonio, Texas, December 9–14, 1968. U.S. GPO, Washington, D.C.

United States Commission on Civil Rights: Mexican American Education Study. Report III: *The Excluded Student* (May 1972). U.S. GPO, Washington, D.C.

3

Values

Introduction

The child is really impossible. His mother keeps him home at least one day a week to "help" her. These parents have no respect or appreciation for what we are trying to do for their children. How does she think he is ever going to develop a sense of responsibility if she doesn't make him come to school? And when he is here, he doesn't try to learn anything. He just waits for recess so he can see Mrs. _____. He is always making up to her. She babies him. I refuse to baby him. He has to learn that I'm not going to hand out special favors. And he will speak Spanish all the time if you let him. He doesn't even seem to want to improve his English. It's no wonder most of the other kids don't like him. Now just what am I supposed to do? I have 25 other children to teach too, you know.

Is it any wonder that many Mexican American students and their parents feel alienated from the schools? Many Mexican American students have concluded, on the basis of their experiences in our schools, that they cannot be bicultural and at the same time achieve academic success. Examples of education programs which attempt to give teachers some understanding of the value system of Mexican American culture are exceedingly rare. Teachers have been given little or no understanding of the differences between their own values and those of their Mexican American pupils. These differences must be recognized, and knowledge of them utilized by teachers before Mexican American children can actually have the opportunity to develop as bicultural indiviudals rather than being forced to make a choice between the culture represented by the school and that which he has already experienced.

A major danger inherent in any attempt to describe the value system of an ethnic group is that of stereotyping. This danger is acute in the case of Mexican Americans because most of the information presently available concerning this ethnic group has resulted from studies carried out in communities where residents are strongly identified with Mexican or Spanish rural culture. (For example, see the studies of Clark, 1959; Kluckhohn & Strodtbeck, 1961; Madsen, 1964; Rubel, 1966; Saunders, 1954.)

Many Mexican Americans now live in urban or semiurban environments, and, consequently, are facing many forces which produce many changes in their value systems. These changes, and the diversity which they have augmented, have caused some researchers to shy away from attempts to describe Mexican American culture and values. If, however, one recognizes that there is a common core of values on which Mexican American culture is based–values which, in one way or another, affect the lives of most Mexican Americans– then some descriptive analysis is, indeed, justifiable. Although many Mexican Americans have adopted values of culture which they have encountered in American society, the original core of values remains, albeit in altered form, continuing to affect behavior.

The common core of Mexican American cultural values makes up what Diaz–Guerrero (1972) has identified as the sociocultural premises: those statements that provide the basis for the specific logic of a cultural group—statements that predict how members of a group think, feel, and act.

This chapter is devoted to an attempt to describe these critical
Mexican American values. At this point, we are concerned with those
values that we have labeled "traditional": those that are characteristic of communities which are rural, are located in close proximity
to the Mexican border, and in which the majority of the population
is Mexican American. We choose to describe these values in detail
since residents of traditional communities have been least affected
by other cultures, and since children of these communities are those
most likely to be adversely affected by the exclusivist practices
that schools have adopted toward Mexican American culture. These
values are the nearest approximation available to that core of values
which affect the behavior of Mexican Americans regardless of the
changes that have occurred due to diversity and external variables.
(The variables leading to diversity and a classification system of
communities that describe this diversity are discussed in Chapter 5.)

It will appear obvious that many of the values of traditional Mexican American culture are similar to those of other ethnic groups,
even to those of some American middle-class groups. The point is
not that Mexican American values are radically different from those
of other ethnic groups, but that they differ significantly from those
usually represented in the schools. Where applicable, we have noted
contrasts between traditional Mexican American values and the
values reflected in the culture of the school. Historically, certain
values have been idealized in American life. Adoption of these idealized values by Mexican Americans and other culturally different
children has been assumed necessary by educational personnel in
order for these children to "survive." Teachers and administrators
alike have been heard to say: "If Mexican American children are
to be successful in this society, they must be competitive, assertive,
and learn to look out for number one."

Four Value Clusters

To facilitate discussion of the complex Mexican American value
system, we shall focus on four major value clusters:

1. identification with family, community, and ethnic group
2. personalization of interpersonal relationships

3. status and role definition in family and community

4. Mexican Catholic ideology

Identification with Family, Community, and Ethnic Group

Individuals reared in traditional communities are encouraged to identify with their families and to remain so identified throughout most of their lives. The needs and interests of the individual are considered secondary to those of the family and the individual is expected to defend his family whenever its honor is threatened, to help other members of the family whenever they are in need, and always to be cognizant of the fact that his actions and accomplishments reflect on his family, enhancing its status or hurting its reputation in the community.

Most families in traditional communities have close ties with one another. In fact, most of these families are related by blood, marriage, or religious ceremony (for example, the practice of having a member of one family become a *padrino* or *madrina* to a member of another family in baptism, confirmation, first communion, or marriage). Since many of the families in the community are related to one another, individuals reared in traditional communities develop identification with the community itself. The community, in other words, is the extended family for the individual.

The histories of families in traditional communities, and in many cases the histories of the communities themselves, are usually tied to the history of the ethnic group. Many families of traditional communities can trace their histories to Mexico, Spain, or directly to pioneers who participated in the Spanish and Mexican settlement of the Southwest. Likewise, many communities with large Mexican American populations (San Antonio, Texas; Monterey, California; and Santa Fe, New Mexico, for example) have made major contributions to the Hispanic history of the states of the Southwest. In traditional communities, the history of the ethnic group is passed on to the younger members of the community by the older members. Much of the history of the Mexican revolution is told by grandparents to younger children. This sense of historical continuity is a major factor in the development of a strong sense of identification with the ethnic group.

Identification with the ethnic group in traditional communities is reflected in the spirit of *La Raza,* the belief that all people of Hispanic descent are united by a common spiritual bond. In other words, all Hispanic people belong to the same extended family and the actions of individual members reflect on the honor of the entire group. Whenever a member of the group becomes successful, he is expected to help others in the group who are in need. The individual who shirks this responsibility is considered a traitor, a *vendido,* a *tio taco.*

The proximity of Mexico to the United States is a powerful factor in reinforcing ethnic identity in Mexican Americans of traditional communities. Loyalty to the ethnic group is strengthened by pressure exerted by friends and relatives in Mexico. Mexican Americans who cannot speak Spanish fluently or whose behavior reflects mainstream American values are labeled *pochos* by Mexicans.

The results of a recent study in Houston, Texas (Ramírez & Price-Williams, 1971) demonstrated the tenacity with which Mexican Americans maintain values related to identification with family and ethnic group. (These results are even more impressive when one considers that Houston is a large urban center and cannot be considered a traditional community.) Mexican American and Anglo–American[1] mothers of fourth-grade children in Catholic parochial schools were interviewed with a questionnaire which assessed attitudes toward child rearing. Items showing the largest differences in agreement between mothers of the two cultural groups are listed in Table 3.1.

American Sense of Separate Identity
Identification with family, community, and ethnic group contrasts with the emphasis that the culture represented in most schools places on a sense of separate identity. Witkin, Dyk, Faterson, Goodenough, and Karp (1962) define this sense of separate identity as:

> . . . the outcome of a person's development of awareness of his own needs, feelings, and attributes, and his identification of these as dis-

[1] The majority of the Anglo mothers were Caucasians who were no longer identified with any ethnic group. A few were second and third generation German or Polish Americans.

TABLE 3.1

Family Values

	Percent of agreement	
	Mexican American	Anglo–American
If parents have a culture of a background different from that of the majority of people in the United States, they should try to keep it and pass it on to their children.	80	56
Relatives are more important than friends.	66	31
It is a good idea for a child to have some friends whose backgrounds are different from his own.	42	89
For a child, loyalty to his family should come above all else.	84	71
Children who work should turn their money over to their parents.	70	22

tinct from the needs, feelings, and attributes of others. A sense of separate identity implies experience of the self as segregated [p. 134].

This value is emphasized by schools. The child is considered as separate from his parents, is treated as a separate entity altogether. Identification with family and community are not emphasized; identification with the ethnic group is discouraged. The fear that continued identification with the ethnic group will lead to feelings of nationalism is evident in curriculum, personnel attitudes, and the classroom environments of most schools. The Mexican American child is encouraged to discard those values related to pride in his ethnic origins and, when asked about his ethnic background, is prompted to respond that he is *American.*

Personalization of Interpersonal Relationships

Interpersonal relationships in traditional Mexican American communities are characterized by openness, warmth, and commitment to mutual dependence. Considerable emphasis is placed on the individual's skill in relating to others, on the development of sensitivity to others' feelings and needs.

The most important characteristic of interpersonal relationships is the commitment to mutual help that results in cooperative achievement among members of traditional communities. There exists in the community the unspoken knowledge that the interest of one is that of all, and, consequently, any assistance offered will be repaid. That is, the concerns of the community, of family and friends, are viewed by the individual as his own. Achievements are rarely viewed as individual achievements, but rather as the result of cooperative efforts. This personalization in traditional communities reinforces the cohesiveness of the community and of the ethnic group.

The need of Mexican American children to establish close ties with others was evident in some of the data collected in the Houston study described earlier. The School Situations Picture Stories Technique (SSPST, see Appendix A, p. 159), a modification of the Thematic Apperception Test, was administered to the fourth-grade children. Each child was asked to tell a story for each of seven picture cards. The stories were then scored for need affiliation[2] (to draw near and enjoyably cooperate with another; to adhere and remain loyal to a friend). Mexican American children scored significantly higher $(\bar{X} = 6.98)$ than Anglo–American children $(\bar{X} = 4.57)$. Analysis of stories elicited by cards depicting children interacting with parents or teachers revealed that Mexican Americans $(\bar{X} = 5.21)$ also scored higher than Anglos $(\bar{X} = 3.49)$ on need succorance (need to have the sympathetic aid of another). Mexican American children expressed greater need for guidance, direction, and support from authority figures. (See also Chapter 4, pp. 59–81.)

Individual Competitive Achievement

The mutual dependence and cooperative achievement characteristic of interpersonal relationships in traditional Mexican American culture contrasts with the achievement through individual competition encouraged by the culture of the schools. This type of competi-

[2] The McClelland (1953) scoring system as revised by Ricciuti and Clark (1957) was used. One point was given for each of four categories: imagery, instrumental activity, positive outcome of instrumental activity, and thema.

tion is related to the sense of separate identity discussed earlier in this chapter. Since the child sees himself as separate from others, he achieves for himself and views himself as the sole possessor of the rewards he achieves. This type of competition not only excludes others from sharing in the rewards, but also has the effect of forcing the individual to view his peers as rivals. Comparing the competitive behavior of Mexican and Anglo children, Nelson and Kagan (1972) state:

> Anglo–American children are not only irrationally competitive, they are almost sadistically rivalrous. Given a choice, Anglo–American children took toys away from their peers 78 percent of the trials even when they could not keep the toys for themselves. . . . Anglo–American children often were willing to make sacrifices in order to reduce the rewards of their peers. . . . Results indicated that with age, an Anglo–American child, significantly more so than a Mexican child, is willing to reduce his own reward in order to reduce the reward of a peer [p. 91].

Status and Role Definition in Family and Community

The concepts *respeto* and *bien educado* illustrate the esteem held in traditional Mexican American communities for role and status definition. Age and sex are important determinants of roles and status. Older people hold more status and are accorded more respect than other members of the community; they are respected for their knowledge of the history of the community and ethnic group, and for having had more experience in life. Parents in particular are accorded much respect. Children are expected to model themselves closely after their parents.

Within the family structure, roles are assigned in accordance with age. The eldest child is usually given more responsibility—status being determined by how well responsibilities are fulfilled. In large families, it is common for older children to be responsible for the socialization of younger siblings.

Children and young adults who are well-behaved are referred to as *bien educados*. To be well-educated socially is considered as important and at times even more important than being well-educated academically. Children who behave properly in social situations and fulfill the responsibilities of their roles give honor to their family in the community.

Separation of the sex roles is emphasized in traditional communities. Males have more status in business and politics, while women have more status in child rearing, health care, and religion. Social scientists who have written about Mexican American culture have overemphasized the concept of *machismo* in the culture, and have generally ignored the reinforcement given for fulfilling the responsibilities of the female role. The mother's role of guiding and supporting children is most important. Females are also expected to provide emotional and spiritual support for the family and to keep the concept of *familia* or extended family alive and functional. (Recent years have witnessed considerable change in the area of separation of the sex roles, even in some traditional communities. Women are becoming increasingly involved in politics while men are taking a greater interest in education.)

Table 3.2 contains those items concerning status and role definition on which Mexican American and Anglo–American mothers in Houston showed greatest disagreement.

TABLE 3.2

Family Values

	Percent of agreement	
	Mexican American	Anglo– American
It is not good for a parent to treat a child as an equal, because he might lose his respect.	77	42
Whenever there are adults visiting, children should not participate in the conversation.	92	53
A child should not be allowed to rebel against his parents' demands.	88	72
Children should be discouraged from playing with toys not appropriate to their sex.	67	31

Mexican Catholic Ideology

Mexican Catholic ideology represents an amalgamation of European and Indian religious ideas and practices. It is a mestizo religious ideology with a mestizo patron saint, the Virgin of Guadalupe. Mexican Catholicism provides support and reinforcement for the values of the three clusters discussed earlier. Identification with ethnic group is reinforced through the worship of the Virgin of Guadalupe, the religious symbol of La Raza. She represents the amalgamation of the European and Indian worlds to form a new people, a new culture.

Identification with the community is reinforced by the emphasis on interfamily ties through religious ceremonies. Identification with the family is encouraged through threat of punishment for disobedience or for placing self-interests before family interests. The individual is encouraged to make adjustments to the demands of the family and society. Parents and other adults are viewed as representatives of God, and to disobey them represents a transgression against God. Young persons are considered to be very susceptible to sin and are therefore given much guidance.

Data from the Houston study provides evidence of these values. Mexican Americans ($\bar{X} = 3.79$) scored higher than Anglo–Americans ($\bar{X} = 2.43$) on need guidance (need to be advised and directed) in the SSPST.

In summary, socialization in traditional Mexican American culture results in individuals who are strongly identified with their families and ethnic group, sensitive to the feelings of others, oriented towards cooperative achievement, respectful of adults and social convention, and who expect to receive close guidance from adults.

The following sketch was selected from among several written at the request of the authors by Mexican American college students who had been reared in traditional Mexican American communities. We have chosen to include this particular essay because the experiences described illustrate in dramatic detail some of the values we have discussed.

My father first came to the United States from Mexico as a teenager to work in the salt mines of Utah and then later he came to this community where he became a self-employed gardener. When I was about 8 or 9, my father began to take my brother and me to work with him after school, and on Saturdays and during summer vacation we would work with my father all day.

As children we did not receive pay for our work because we were expected to contribute to the support of the family.

My father would always come home from work to have lunch and so during the summer months our family would all have lunch together. Sometimes when we were more pressed for time, my mother would prepare lunch at home and then bring it to us where we were working.

Many times, especially when we had a lot of extra work, my mother would leave her own work at home and come out to help us so that on several occasions our whole family became involved with my father's work.

My brother and I continued to work with our father through elementary and high school and even into the first years of college; and even now that our father is semiretired, I continue to help him from time to time.

Our grandparents' home which was within walking distance from our own home was the focal point in the community for our family. We grandchildren frequently stayed at our grandmother's for the weekends. My cousins and I all used to look foward to this because at night my grandmother would sit on the floor with us and tell many different cuentos *or stories about persons and places in Mexico. The stories I remember most are the ones about* La Llorona, *the* Virgen de Guadalupe, *and about the Indians of Mexico and all the knowledge they had, especially about medicine and plants. I also remember her telling stories about how in Mexico a man's arm had withered away because he rose it against his father, and also of other people who were swallowed up by the earth for lying to their parents.*

My grandmother, in her tales about Mexico, talked very much about religious things, especially the Virgen de Guadalupe *and* El Santo Niño de Atocha. *She also spoke about how villages in Mexico named after some saint would have large fiestas lasting a week or longer in commemoration of their patron saint.*

My grandmother used to tell us the story of how in 1907 my grandfather and her and three of my grandfather's cousins and their fami-

lies all left their small village in Mexico and set out for the United States. She said that my grandfather and his cousins had signed up as laborers for the Santa Fe railroad and that for the next 14 years they had all traveled together across the United States working on the railroads. She said that during that time the railroads had brought over thousands of families from Mexico to work for them and that these families were scattered all over the country.

In 1922 my grandfather brought his family to California and settled in this community where some of our relatives already lived. As time went on my grandmother said that more of our relatives from Mexico also came to live in this community after hearing from my grandfather that there was work available in the citrus industry. I was born about 30 years after my grandparents and their family, which included my mother, came to this community and by that time about one-third of the community was related. Our family ties also extended into many families in the community by means of the compadrazco and my grandmother tells of she and my grandfather having somewhere around 60 or 70 sets of compadres *in the community.*

After my grandmother finished telling us stories we would all kneel and then she would come around to each one of us, (there were usually six or seven of us) and make the sign of the cross on our forehead. She would then call my grandfather and together they would give us their blessing after which we would rise and go over to kiss our grandparents' right hand. Then we would all sleep on the living room floor, using as mattresses the thick colchas *or quilts which my grandmother made. My grandmother would usually sleep with us on the floor, but my grandfather would always sleep on the bed.*

People in the community often came to my grandparents for advice and some would come to ask for their blessing before leaving on a trip. Some people also came to my grandmother when someone in their family had susto, *which is like a state of shock usually brought on by some traumatic experience. The treatment for* susto *which my grandmother used required the person to lie down and hold a holy medal or small crucifix at their chest. She would then recite a special prayer nine times while brushing the body of the person in a sweeping motion from head to toe with freshly cut leaves of a rosemary bush. The person would then stand up and recite some prayers after my grandmother while holding the rosemary leaves at their chest. I remember that my grandmother once treated me for* susto *as a child when I had been frightened at night by a dog that tried to bite me and that after her treatment I felt a great lessening of my fear.*

Not everyone can successfully treat susto *because the treatment requires special prayers which are usually known only by a few holy people and because the prayers of those holy people are more readily heard by God.*

Also, when someone in the community died, the family of the deceased would often ask one of these devout persons to come to their home and to lead the family in reciting the rosary and other special prayers in memory of the deceased. This took place for nine evenings after the funeral, and the devout person would, of course, never take anything in return for his or her services. When my grandfather died, my grandmother and her eldest daughter led our family in praying the rosary.

Our parents used to visit our grandparents every day and help them with any work which there might be around their house. We were also taken along to our grandparents' home every day and ran errands to the store or to other places for them, and helped out with other chores. As time went on we grandchildren were gradually given more responsibility for our grandparents' welfare so that today we still visit our grandmother daily and take her to the doctor or to church, do her marketing for her and do any other work needed around the house, such as painting or gardening. My aunts and female cousins get together often and clean house for my grandmother. Even if there is nothing which needs to be done around her house we still come over just to talk with her, keep her company and give her any news about the family. On Sunday mornings, after Mass, my father takes over to my grandmother's a large kettle of menudo *and two dozen* tortillas *and our family, usually including some uncles and aunts, eats Sunday breakfast together at her house, as it has been done so even since before I was born.*

In our community our church was totally Mexican and so as a child I did not distinguish between Catholic and Mexican. I thought that Christ and his Apostles were Mexican people and that if you were not Mexican you could not be Catholic. It came as a surprise to find out that Blacks and Anglos could also be Catholic.

As children our grandparents and parents taught us special prayers for different occasions, and many of these prayers are not found in English. They taught us also about the different saints and how a particular saint could be prayed to in order to receive his help for some problem in life for which that saint was recognized to be adept in solving. In our church, the Virgen de Guadalupe occupied a very special place and not only our parents and grandparents but the priests as well taught us that we as Mexicanos should feel honored and proud that God had sent His own mother to be the patroness de Nuestra Raza (of our people). In our home and in our grandparents' home there is a small shrine for the Virgin at which a candle is always kept lit.

During the month of May our family would pray the rosary together at night before the Virgin's shrine and then afterwards my brother and I would receive our parents' blessing and then kiss their right hand as a sign of respect for them. My brother and I would then extend our hand to our parents and help them to get up from their kneeling position.

As youngsters my brother and I were both Altar boys at our church. In our community being an Altar boy was like belonging to a boys club because not only did we serve at Mass but also we got to go on outings. The church therefore provided about the only source of recreation for Chicano boys in the community at that time.

The church in our community was a central gathering place for much of the community. During the days before Christmas there used to be Posadas at the church and the people would walk in procession with little candles through some of the streets in the community. After the services there would be a piñata in the church courtyard for the children who had participated in the services. Also, on the feast of La Virgen de Guadalupe, there would be Mañanitas at our church and the mariachis would play outside the church at sunrise and also after the Mass. When the mariachis were done playing at the church, they would come over to our grandparents home for breakfast and then afterwards they would stay for a while and play for everyone at the house.

On the Cinco de Mayo *and the* 16 de Septiembre *our church would hold small fiestas in the church courtyard and so traditional national holidays also became associated with the church.*

Although there were many festivities which took place at our church, the message which came down from the pulpit on Sunday was a serious one. Our priest, who was Mexican, very strongly emphasized strict obedience to God's law. Respeto *and* obediencia *were the themes of many sermons and the priests used to stress that just as we obeyed and respected God's law, that we should obey and respect parents and elders because God had given them authority over us. To be disrespectful and disobedient to our parents, therefore, was as if we had done this to God Himself.*

As children our parents taught us always to have the greatest respect for our grandparents. We were taught always to kiss our grandparents' right hand whenever we entered their home and to ask for their blessing, which we received while kneeling, when leaving their home. We were also taught to answer our grandparents and all other adults with the phrase "mande usted" *when we were called by them. To respond to an adult by simply saying* "que" *or* "what" *was considered disrespectful and indicative of the fact that the person had not been* bien educado *but was instead a* mal criado *[badly raised child]. To have a child who was considered by others to be* mal criado *was a disgrace on the parents and family of that child.*

If my brother and I were ever disrespectful to our elders we could count on being punished by our father and usually in the form of a whipping with his belt. However, before we received our punishment my mother would have us kneel before our father and ask him for his forgiveness. This did not mean that we were going to be spared the whipping but rather it was sign to acknowledge that we respected him even under such unpleasant conditions.

My mother would always (and still does) refer us to my grandfather and father for us to imitate when correcting our behavior by saying something like "why don't you learn from your father, he would never do anything like that" *(in Spanish) or* "your grandfather would be hurt if he knew what you did."

Our parents emphasized that we should never talk back to our elders and that we should treat other adults as if they were our own parents. If my brother and I were going out somewhere with the family of some friends my father would always tell the parents of our friends "hay te los encargo," meaning "I put them in your charge." We understood that as long as we were with that family, those parents had complete authority over us just as if they were our own parents and that we should obey and respect them accordingly.

As children our parents would not only tell us that we should be helpful to others, but also conveyed this message to us through their own example. For instance, I remember that in our neighborhood my mother was one of the very few women who drove a car and so she would drive many of the ladies, especially the older ones, to their doctor appointments, the market, church or to visit relatives in the hospital or jail. My mother would never take anything in return for her services unless she saw that she might hurt someone's feelings by not accepting what they had to offer in return.

My father, like my mother, also gave us good example through his actions. I remember that when some relative or friend was out of work, that he would hire them as a helper even though he really didn't need the help. This, of course, meant that our family's income was lessened because he had to pay the helper, but my father used to say that he was grateful for the fact that he always had work and that our family had enough and that we should do whatever we could to help others who were less fortunate, especially if they were related to the family.

Our parents were very concerned that my brother and I should get a good education which taught us not only about things in books but also about having respect for others. For this reason, among others, our parents sent us to the Catholic school for most of our elementary school education. This put a financial hardship on our parents but they said that such a sacrifice was an obligation which they had as parents. Our parents were also concerned that we should get a good education in our religion.

Another thing which motivated our parents to send us to the parochial school was the attitude of the public school which we first went to and which was just across the street from our house. The teachers there, although usually nice, would make very little effort to encourage the students who were all Mexican except for a few blacks. I guess they thought we probably weren't interested in learn-

ing and so they made little effort to really teach us anything. Instead, I remember, they would keep us occupied with a lot of things like building blocks and water colors.

Our parents were, in addition, concerned about the reports that the teachers would send home about my brother and me. My mother still talks about the one report in which the teacher remarked that my brother was a very slow learner, too quiet and was also a day- dreamer, but that otherwise he was a very nice little boy and so not to worry about him. Our parents felt that if we continued at the same school we might always remain slow learners and so decided to send us to the Catholic school where the nuns, although much stricter, were more concerned that we actually learn something and gave us much more encouragement.

Conclusions

The differences between Mexican American and other American cultures constitute a reality which many Mexican American children face daily. In school, they find that the expectations of educational personnel are unrelated to their early experience. For example, the Mexican American child may go to school speaking Spanish and having pride in his Mexican background, and find that he is not allowed to speak Spanish and that his background is considered inferior. He may go to school wanting to achieve for his family, but discover that his parents are not encouraged to participate in the educational process. He may go to school with a cooperative achievement orientation and find that individual competition is en- couraged. He may go with the expectation of establishing close personal ties with his teachers, of modeling himself after his teachers, and encounter teachers who are detached, who do not act as close guides. Perhaps most damaging of all is the feeling that he must reject his culture in order to be accepted. Since he is viewed as different or disadvantaged when he behaves according to the norms of Mexican American culture, he comes to perceive that ac- ceptance and success are predicated upon behaving like a member of the mainstream American middle class. For this child, the result is confusion. He feels a loss of orientation and, eventually, rejection.

Little wonder that absenteeism and dropout rates are so high for Mexican Americans.

The development of teachers' understanding of Mexican American values is one of the primary concerns of educators attempting to provide culturally democratic educational environments. Equally important is provision of information concerning the nature and use of learning styles in the classroom. The conceptual framework of cognitive styles is unique in that, while it is to a great degree determined by values and socialization practices, it subsumes other variables, including patterns of motivation and human–relational styles—and may, therefore, be used to transform theory into practice. Chapter 4 is devoted to a discussion of cognitive styles and related variables, followed in Chapter 5 by an analysis of the intimate relationships between cognition, values, and socialization practices.

Summary

Mexican American children experience difficulty in school because their culture is not given recognition in the classroom and because school personnel are not aware of differences between traditional Mexican American and mainstream American middle-class cultures. The sociocultural system of traditional Mexican American culture is composed of four major value clusters: (1) identification with family, community, and ethnic group; (2) personalization of interpersonal relationships; (3) status and role definition in family and community; and (4) Mexican Catholic ideology. Mainstream American middle-class values most often represented in schools can be categorized under the value clusters: (1) sense of separate identity; and (2) individual competitive achievement.

References

Clark, M. *Health in the Mexican–American culture: A community study*. Berkeley, California: Univ. of California Press, 1959.
Diaz-Guerrero, R. *Hacia una teoria historico—biopsico—sociocultural del comportamiento humano*. Mexico: Editorial Trillas, 1972.

Kluckhohn, F., & Strodtbeck, F. *Variations in value orientations.* New York: Harper, 1961.

Madsen, W. *Mexican Americans of south Texas.* New York: Holt, 1964.

McClelland, D. C., Atkinson, J. W., Clark, R. A., & Lowell, E. L. *The achievement motive.* New York: Appleton, 1953.

Nelson, L. L., & Kagan, S. Competition: The star-spangled scramble. *Psychology Today,* 1972, **6**(4), 53–56, 90–91.

Ramírez III, M., & Price-Williams, D. The relationship of culture to educational attainment. Center for Research in Social Change and Economic Development, Houston, Texas: Rice Univ., 1971.

Ricciuti, H. N., & Clark, R. A. A comparison of need-achievement stories written by "relaxed" and "achievement oriented" subjects: Effects obtained with new pictures and revised scoring categories. Princeton, New Jersey: Educational Testing Service, 1957.

Rubel, A. J. *Across the tracks: Mexican Americans in a Texas city.* Austin, Texas: Univ. of Texas Press, 1966.

Saunders, L. *Cultural difference and medical care: The case of the Spanish-speaking people of the southwest.* New York: Russell Sage Foundation, 1954.

Witkin, H. A., Dyk, R. B., Faterson, H. F., Goodenough, D. R., & Karp, S. A. *Psychological differentiation.* New York: Wiley, 1962.

4

Cognitive Styles

Introduction

A child should be encouraged to be very competitive.

Children should be allowed to do things on their own so that they can learn from their mistakes.

A mother should protect her child as much as possible because he/she will have plenty of time later to face reality and suffering.

Children should be guided very closely by their parents so they do not make as many mistakes and become discouraged.

The four statements above were taken from a socialization measure used in a study in Houston with Mexican American and Anglo–American mothers (Ramírez & Price–Williams, 1974b). The first two items received more positive responses from the Anglo–American mothers, while the third and fourth statements

59

Figure 4.1.   *Relationship of culture to cognitive styles.*

received more positive responses from Mexican American mothers. The differences in attitudes illustrated in these findings
are reflected in socialization practices of the two cultures. Socialization styles, including teaching approaches, the nature of rewards, and characteristics of the relationship between "teacher"
and learner, which children experience at home, differ from culture to culture. Values and socialization styles determine or affect
development of cognitive style in children, and differences which
parallel those seen in socialization practices may be seen in several areas of behavior (see Figure 4.1).

Through socialization practices children develop preferences for
certain types of rewards—certain rewards have more meaning for
them—and, consequently, the learner is more motivated by culturally appropriate incentives. Children's behavior is also affected
by the manner in which they have learned to relate with the person
in the teaching role. This human–relational style in preschool
learning is one which the child expects to be continued in the
school setting. Furthermore, children develop their own styles of
learning, their own modes of organizing, classifying, and assimilating information about their environments (i.e., learning set).
Thus, values, through socialization practices, affect many school
and learning behaviors which, when recognized, may be utilized
to teach children effectively.

Incentive–Motivational Styles

Among the behaviors of Mexican American and Anglo–American
children which have been studied is incentive–motivational style
as it is manifested in competition. Using an instrument designed

to investigate cooperation and competition, Kagan and Madsen (1971) studied the behavior of Mexican, Mexican American, and Anglo–American children. When the children were asked to cooperate with each other to achieve rewards, Mexican and Mexican American children were more cooperative than Anglo–American children. When the experimenter gave the children a competitive set on the same task; Anglo–American children were more competitive than either Mexican or Mexican American children. The Mexican American children were more highly motivated in the cooperative setting than in the competitive.

In another study (Ramírez & Price–Williams, 1974c) which further illustrates differences in incentive–motivational style, stories told by Mexican American and Anglo–American children to the School Situations Picture Stories Technique (SSPST, see Appendix A, p. 159). were analyzed for need achievement. Anglo–American children scored higher on need achievement (as defined by McClelland, Atkinson, Clark, & Lowell, 1953) and Mexican American children scored higher on need achievement *for the family*. That is, stories told by Mexican American children indicated that they wanted to achieve so that their parents would be proud of them or so that their family might benefit from their achievements. In contrast, stories told by Anglo–American children reflected need achievement for self, in which the achiever is the primary beneficiary.

The following stories told by Mexican American children include examples of need achievement for the family.

This boy wants to be a success so that he can help his family. He feels he owes a lot to his parents, and he also wants to help his brothers and sisters go to college. Every night he studies hard. He does not watch TV or go out with his friends. In the end he goes to college and becomes a famous engineer. His parents are proud of him and he can help everyone in his family.

This girl is Janie. She never likes to do her work in school. The teacher scolds her but she doesn't pay attention. She just fools around with her friends and she daydreams. One day the teacher talks to the principal and they give Janie a note. The note tells her parents that they have to come to school. Janie comes to school

*with her parents and they are talking to Mrs. Jones and to Mr.
Thomas, the principal. Mrs. Jones and Mr. Thomas tell her parents
how Janie never does her work. Her parents say, "Janie, you must
study and get good grades. We want you to be a good student. That
is very important." Janie feels good and she wants to make her
parents proud. She tries real hard and makes all A's.*

Human–Relational Styles

Another study with the SSPST (Ramírez & Price–Williams, 1974d),
focusing this time on human–relational styles, showed that Mexican
Americans scored higher on need affiliation (indicating a greater
desire to interact with others and belong to a social group) and on
need to nurture (showing greater sensitivity to others' feelings and
a willingness to help others). These qualities seem to develop from
the emphasis on personalization of interpersonal relationships in the
culture, an indication of the emphasis which is given to the social
environment (see Chapter 3, pp. 44–45). Mexican American children
also scored high on need succorance (willingness to rely on others,
particularly adults, for help and guidance). The stories showed a tendency to view authority figures as benevolent guides who are gen-
uinely interested in one's welfare. Mexican American children also
indicated in the stories a desire to become "just like" a teacher,
parent, or other respected adult. The need for succorance emanates
in part from the influence of Mexican Catholic ideology (see Chapter
3, p. 48). The following are sample stories reflecting need affiliation
and need succorance, respectively, which were told by Mexican
American children:

*This girl, Mary, is new at the school. She wants to be friends with
the other girls. She is very lonely right now and wonders how she
can get the girls to like her. One day one of the most popular girls,
Peggy, has trouble with her math. Mary helps her and then everyone
likes her and they let her play with them.*

*Rosie admires her teacher very much. She wants to be like her
some day. She hopes she will be able to help other children like
her teacher does. Her teacher, Mrs. Jay, always gives Rosie good*

advice and helps her when she can't do things good in school. Rosie
likes to be with her and she likes it when Mrs. Jay helps her. Rosie
is a good student because Mrs. Jay cares about her. When Rosie
goes to college, she visits Mrs. Jay and says thank you for helping
me always.

Patterns of Intellectual Abilities and Learning Styles

Other studies have identified differences between Mexican American and Anglo–American children on variables directly related to cognitive functioning. Research recently completed in Houston, Texas (Ramírez & Price–Williams, 1971) compared the performance of Mexican American and Anglo–American children on a series of tasks. Fourth-grade children enrolled in Catholic parochial schools were asked to tell stories to picture cards depicting educational scenes (SSPST). Analysis of these stories revealed that those related by Mexican American children were lengthier, indicative of greater verbal productivity, and included more characters than those related by Anglo–American children.

These children were also asked to free associate to the names of their three best friends. They were shown the names one at a time and allowed 10 seconds to respond. Mexican American children gave more associations per name than did Anglo–American children. Moreover, subsequent analysis revealed that those associations given by Mexican American children could be classified into a greater number of categories, such as physical appearance, academic abilities, social abilities, and dress.

On still another task (Beman, 1972), the children were tested with Piaget's tasks for conservation of mass, weight, and volume. Anglo–American children conserved better in all three areas than did Mexican American children.

These findings showing that Mexican American and Anglo–American children differ in their patterns of performance support the general contention that differences in culture are associated with differences in patterns of intellectual performance. Similar findings have been obtained by Lesser, Fifer, and Clark (1965) and Stodolsky and Lesser (1967). They, too, determined that members of different ethnic groups exhibit different patterns of intellectual performance, each group achieving better in some areas than in others. These patterns were similar for children of different socioeconomic groups within the same cultural group. Their conclusions resulted from testing American children of four cultural groups: Chinese, Jewish, Black, and Puerto Rican. Jewish children performed best on tasks of verbal ability, but had difficulty on tasks of space conceptualization, while the reverse was true for Chinese children.

Stodolsky and Lesser (1967) explain these results by stating: "Different kinds of intellectual skills are fostered or hindered in different cultural environments [p. 562]." This seems to imply that experiences with certain tasks and differential reinforcement result in a facility for doing some tasks and an inability to perform adequately on others. For example, Mexican American culture emphasizes sensitivity to the social environment, thus, Mexican American children perform well on tasks requiring free association to the names of their peers.

We would hypothesize that these differences in intellectual patterns are also due to culturally determined learning styles: modes of organizing, classifying, and assimilating information about the environment which are unique to each cultural group. Cohen (1969) refers to these as "integrated rule-sets for the selection and organization of sense data [p. 836]."

All of the research reviewed here indicates that culture produces unique behaviors which affect the performance of children in school. What is needed is an all-encompassing concept that can account for all these behaviors and thus make it possible to implement cultural democracy effectively.

Cognitive Styles

The much-needed conceptual framework emerged from some of the findings of the Houston study (Ramírez & Price–Williams, 1974a). Data collected with cognitive tests showed that, in general, Mexican American children tended to be more field dependent in cognitive style, whereas Anglo–American children were more likely to be of the field-independent style. The terms "field dependent" and "field independent" were first described by Witkin, Dyk, Faterson, Good-enough, and Karp (1962) and emerged from their research on per-ception. In a field-dependent mode of perception, the organization of the field as a whole dominates perception of its parts; an item within a field is experienced as fused with the organized ground. In a field-independent mode of perception, the person is able to per-ceive items as discrete from the organized field. This concept en-compasses a wide range of intellectual and affective variables. For example, field-dependent children do best on verbal tasks of intel-ligence tests; learn materials more easily which have human, social content, and which are characterized by fantasy and humor; are sen-sitive to the opinions of others; perform better when authority figures express confidence in their ability; and, conversely, perform less well when authority figures doubt their ability. Field-independent children do best on analytic tasks; learn material that is inanimate and impersonal more easily; and their performance is not greatly affected by the opinions of others (Cohen, 1969; Messick, 1970; Ramírez, 1973).

It is reasonable to assume that the concept can also be helpful in implementing cultural democracy in the classroom. Cohen (1969), for example, has found that most school environments reflect the field-independent style, the style unfamiliar to most Mexican Ameri-can children. In light of our findings, this would mean that these schools are inappropriate (undemocratic) for most Mexican Ameri-can children. Since field dependence/field independence will be-come one of the focal points for development of culturally demo-cratic educational environments, the history of its development merits review.

Field Dependence/Field Independence

History and Measurement

The research of Witkin et al. (1962) on field dependence/field in-dependence had a somewhat unusual beginning. During World War II it was observed that when pilots lost sight of the ground they would frequently lose their sense of the upright, and fly upside down or sideways. Witkin's early work focused on the characteristic ways

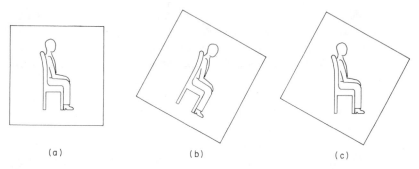

(a)   (b)   (c)

Figure 4.2. *Body Adjustment Test: (a) room and chair vertical; (b) room and chair tilted; (c) chair vertical, room tilted.*

in which people perceive both the world and themselves. One of the early test situations developed by Witkin was the Body Adjustment Test which consisted of a movable chair in a simulated room suspended on ball-bearing pivots (see Figure 4.2). The subject was blindfolded and seated in the chair which could be tilted independently of the room. The room and chair were then tilted, and the blindfold removed. The subject was asked to return his body to the true upright while the room remained tilted. The subject told the experimenter the direction in which to move the chair to return it to the upright.

In another task, the subject was seated in a completely darkened room facing a luminous rod enclosed by a luminous frame. The rod and frame were tilted, and the subject was asked to set the rod to the true vertical position while the frame remained tilted. A significant correlation was noted between the two tests: The subject who had difficulty with the Body Adjustment Test also had difficulty adjusting the rod to the upright position. The differences observed in individual performance on these two tasks were initially thought to be due to individual differences on the extent of reliance on visual cues obtained from the environment as opposed to internal cues obtained from the subject's own body. That is, some people relied on the external cues to reach a decision regarding the true upright while others relied on the internal cues.

Later investigations showed that subjects who had difficulty overcoming the influence of the tilted frame or room also had difficulty overcoming the influence of complex designs when asked to find a part of that design in an Embedded Figures Test. In this test the subject is shown a simple figure, like a triangle, and then asked to find the figure in a more complex geometrical design (see Figures 4.3 and 4.4).

The interpretation of external versus internal orientation, then, extended to a more general dimension of perceptual analysis. This extended conception of the dimension was then labeled field dependence/field independence. The perception of a relatively field-dependent subject is dominated by the overall organization of the field, whereas relatively field-independent subjects readily perceive elements as discrete from their backgrounds, from the totality of which they are a part.

The Embedded Figures Tests (both child and adult forms) and the Portable Rod and Frame Test (Oltman, 1968) are currently the most widely used instruments to assess cognitive style. These two particular instruments have rapidly gained in popularity among researchers because they have the advantages of being more portable and simpler to administer than either the Body Adjustment Test or original Rod and Frame apparatus. The Portable Rod and Frame Test consists of a long rectangularly shaped box constructed of translucent white plastic and rests on a table. The child is asked to position his head at one end of the box. Directly in front of him he sees a black frame and a black rod—both the rod and the frame can be turned independently of each other. The experimenter raises a screen in front of the subject's eyes, and then moves the rod and frame 28° off the vertical. He then lowers the screen and asks the subject to tell him in which direction to move the rod to return it to its vertical position. He warns the subject that the frame will remain tilted so that he ought not guide himself by the tilt of the frame. Subjects are given eight trials, and the score is the average number of degrees error over the eight trials (see Figure 4.5).

As in the case of the Body Adjustment Test apparatus, field-dependent individuals appear to depend on the frame to make their decision concerning the verticality of the rod, thus leaving the rod tilted—most often in the direction of the tilt of the frame.

The Draw—a—Person Test has also been used to assess cognitive style. Discussion of the different instruments for assessing cognitive

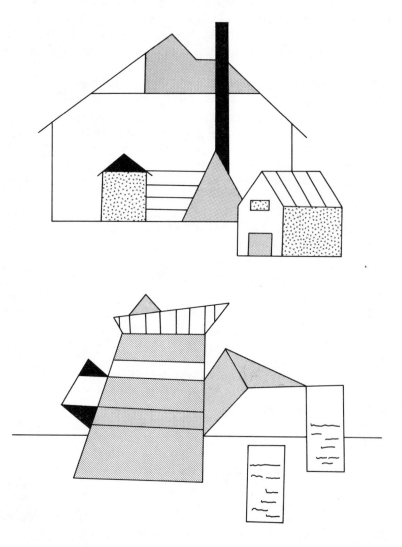

Figure 4.3. *Samples from Children's Embedded Figures Test. Each pattern in this reproduction represents a different color in the actual test (Consulting Psychologists Press, Inc. Palo Alto, California, 1971).*

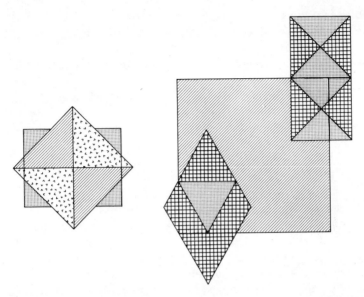

Figure 4.4. *Samples from Embedded Figures Test (adult). Each pattern in this reproduction represents a different color in the actual test (H. A. Witkin, Consulting Psychologists Press, Inc. Palo Alto, California, 1969).*

style and their effectiveness in assessing cognitive style in Mexican American children is contained in Appendix B, pp. 163–165.

The importance of field dependence/field independence becomes increasingly apparent as relationships between this concept and

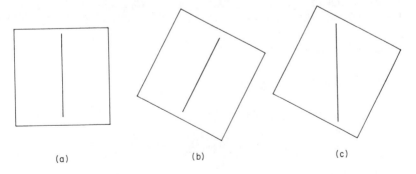

(a)   (b)   (c)

Figure 4.5. *Portable Rod and Frame Test: (a) frame and rod in vertical position; (b) frame and rod tilted; (c) frame tilted, rod vertical.*

variables that are critical to education are identified. The remainder of this chapter will be concerned with these relationships.

Preferred Modes of Thinking, Remembering, Perceiving, and Problem Solving

Work by Witkin and his colleagues (1962), uncovered an interesting pattern of correlations between measures of cognitive styles and different subtests of the Wechsler intelligence scales. The subtests of the Wechsler scales cluster into three major areas: a *verbal* dimension, an *attention–concentration* dimension, and an *analytic* dimension. The only cluster of subtests found to correlate significantly with measures of field dependence/field independence was that of the analytic dimension. Individuals scoring toward the field-independence end of the dimension tended to score higher on such subtests as Block Design, Object Assembly, and Picture Completion. No difference was found between field-dependent and field-independent individuals on the other two subsets of test items. The frequent finding that field-independent individuals tend to score higher on measures of intelligence than field-dependent individuals may be interpreted to indicate an advantage held by field-independent subjects in responding to items of the analytic dimension.

Research by Cohen (1969) has also shown that when the test materials are characterized by an abstract or impersonal nature, field-independent individuals appear to have an advantage. However, a markedly different pattern becomes evident when the test materials focus on social or human factors. Field-dependent individuals also give longer and more complex stories to picture cards designed to assess verbal expressiveness (Witkin *et al.*, 1962). Field-dependent individuals appear to remember faces and social words more often than field-independent individuals, though their incidental memory for nonsocial stimuli is not generally superior (Messick & Damarin, 1964; Fitzgibbons, Goldberger, & Eagle, 1965). Field dependents have also been found to be more effective in tasks or situations that involve relevant social cues (Ruble & Nakamura, 1972).

It appears that in some form or another, field-dependent individuals are more influenced by, or more sensitive to, the human element in the environment. On the other hand, field-independent individuals have an advantage in test situations which deemphasize the human element, situations in which the test material is relatively more impersonal. They are more able to isolate parts from a whole, and are less constrained by conventional uses of objects and materials (Witkin *et al.,* 1962).

Characteristics which differentiate field-dependent from field-independent individuals, then, are those that reflect preferred modes of relating to, classifying, assimilating, and organizing the environment.

Incentive–Motivational Styles

The term, "incentive–motivational style," may be defined as a preference for a set of goals and rewards (incentives). These incentives are represented by changes in the environment which indicate, symbolize, or have become associated with support, acceptance, and positive recognition of behavior. Preferred incentives refer to those sets of environmental events which most effectively influence the behavior of an individual. Of concern here is how effectively different environmental events influence, modify, or reinforce behavior.

Examination of the research into differences in incentive–motivational preferences supports the observation that field-dependent persons are more influenced by the human element in the environment than are field-independent persons.

Approval (praise) exhibited by an authority figure appears to be more effective with field-dependent children than with field-independent children. For example, it has been found that the performance of field-dependent children is depressed when an authority figure indicates disapproval by remarking (Konstadt & Forman, 1965, p. 491), "This doesn't seem like the kind of group that can do well, but you might as well try as long as you're here," or "You're not as fast as our other groups, don't you want to cooperate?"

Conversely, these children are motivated under conditions in which the authority figure indicates approval through praise: "This is a very bright group, you are going to do well on this test," or "You certainly have caught on faster than most children, I can see you will do well [p. 491]." The tendency for field-dependent children to seek approval from the authority figure is consistent with the observation that when stress was introduced into a testing situation, field-dependent children tended to orient, or look up to the face of the adult examiner, about twice as often as field-independent children (Konstadt & Forman, 1965).

One of the differences between the incentive–motivational styles of field-dependent and field-independent individuals is related to the interpersonal dimension. For example, field-dependent individuals are more likely to be motivated by those forms of reward that offer personalized support, recognition, or acceptance.

Human–Relational Styles

Use of the field-dependence/field-independence concept has provided some valuable insights into human–relational styles (preferred modes of relating to others). A study of field-dependent and field-independent psychiatrists (Pollak & Kiev, 1963) indicated that field-independent psychiatrists preferred either a directive instructional approach, or a passive observational approach in relating to patients. Field-dependent psychiatrists, on the other hand, preferred establishing more mutual, personal relationships with their patients. Research on the behavior of patients in psychotherapy has also produced some interesting insights relative to differences in their preferred modes of relating to authority figures (Witkin, 1965). Field-dependent patients have been observed to exhibit the following characteristics: these patients (1) tend to accept the therapist's suggestions more readily; (2) prefer to establish a trust relationship with the therapist before discussing their problems, requiring the therapist to be active and ask questions; (3) experience feelings of separation anxiety toward the end of the therapy hour, making attempts to prolong it; and (4) seem to want to identify with the therapist. In contrast, field-independent patients exhibit the following characteristics: They (1) require more time to form a close relationship with a therapist; (2) usually come to the therapist with an articulated account of their problems; and (3) seem to prefer to have the therapist assume the role of technical resource person or consultant.

The concept of field dependence/field independence provides some interesting and suggestive insights into the dynamics of interpersonal perceptions between student and teacher. In a recent study by DiStefano (1970), five extremely field-independent teachers and five extremely field-dependent teachers were asked to describe 11 students by means of 21 bipolar semantic differential scales and

25 single adjective scales. The students who were described were also classified as field dependent or field independent, and were asked to describe the teachers in the same manner. DiStefano's (1970) main conclusion was that:

> People with similar perceptual styles tend to describe each other in highly positive terms, while people whose perceptual styles are different have a strong tendency to describe each other in negative terms [p. 6].

The research reviewed here, then, indicates that the concept of field dependence/field independence can serve as the conceptual framework linking culture to intellectual and affective behavior in children, as well as a tool for implementing cultural democracy in the classroom. We shall now focus on the relation of culture to field dependence/field independence. (The implementation of cultural democracy through cognitive styles will be presented at length in Chapter 7.)

Witkin's Theory from a Bicultural Perspective

Although Witkin's conceptual framework is valuable in explaining the differences in behavior exhibited by Mexican American and Anglo–American children, some reservations must be mentioned. Altogether too much emphasis has been placed on the presumed advantages of field independence and disadvantages of field dependence. Field-independent socialization practices have been defined in more favorable value-laden terms than field-dependent child-rearing practices (Witkin et al., 1962). Such descriptions make it easy to conclude that some cultures are pathological because they interfere with the development of field-independent characteristics in children. In fact, Witkin's theory of differentiation leads directly to this conclusion. According to Witkin's theory, all people are field dependent or undifferentiated at birth. As they develop they become more field independent or differentiated. The concept of differentiation, then, assumes that field dependence is a more rudimentary stage of development. Such a presumption excludes the possibility that a field-dependent cognitive style may develop independently of a field-independent style. In fact, cross-cultural research (Witkin, 1967) has shown that members of some cultures tend to be field dependent, while people of other cultures tend to be field independent. This would seem to indicate that cultures, through socialization practices, encourage the development of either relatively more field-dependent or field-independent cognitive styles in children. The fact that research shows that children tend to do better on the Portable Rod and Frame and Embedded Figures tests as they grow older *does not exclude the possibility that they may also be continuing to develop in ways appropriate to the field-dependent style, and this may be a more relevant possibility for children growing up in bicultural environments.* While the Portable Rod and Frame and Embedded Figures tests may be adequate measures of field independence our observations show that they do not accurately measure field dependence. Thus, just because a child's performance on the Portable Rod and Frame Test indicates that he is becoming more field independent as he grows older does not necessarily mean that he is becoming less field dependent. Consequently, we see a need to qualify Witkin's theory of differentiation.

The hypothesis that field independence and field dependence are separate cognitive styles is supported by Cohen (1969). She identifies two conceptual styles—analytic and relational—which are similar to field dependence and field independence. Cohen (1969) defines analytic and relational as follows:

> The analytic cognitive style is characterized by a formal or analytic mode of abstracting salient information from a stimulus or situation and by a stimulus-centered orientation to reality, and it is parts-specific (i.e., parts or attributes of a given stimulus have meaning in themselves). The relational cognitive style, on the other hand, requires a descriptive mode of abstraction and is self-centered in its orientation to reality; only the global characteristics of a stimulus have meaning to its users, and these only in reference to some total context [pp. 829–830].

Recent research on brain functioning indicates that each cognitive style may be primarily localized in a different cerebral hemisphere. Characteristics of the field-sensitive cognitive style are analogous to those identified with the functioning of the right cerebral hemisphere, whereas characteristics of the field-independent cognitive style are similar to those identified as functions of the left hemi-sphere. For example, research strongly suggests (TenHouten, 1971) that the left hemisphere dominates the functions of speech, reading, and writing. It is specialized in verbal activity and analytic thought. The right hemisphere, on the other hand, seems to be dominant for certain visuospatial tasks, which include understanding of music and other art forms, shape and face recognition, and thought based on a simultaneous grasp of related but differing phenomena. The most convincing evidence that each cognitive style is localized in a differ-ent cerebral hemisphere comes from studies on split-brained ani-mals and humans. Split-brain refers to that condition whereby the corpus callosum, the bundle of fibers that join the left and right hemispheres of the brain, has been severed. Gazzaniga and Young (1967) have shown that monkeys whose hemispheres have been dis-connected can solve independent problems with each hand simul-taneously, in contrast to unoperated monkeys who have difficulty doing this. Gazzaniga and Sperry (1966) have shown that this same phenomena also holds for human patients who have undergone the same operation. Ornstein (1973) states

> . . . one preliminary experiment with split-brained people shows that their two hemispheres can process more information at once than can those of a normal person [p. 90].

This suggests that man has two separate minds which after their separation can be regarded as two separate spheres of consciousness.

Not only does it appear that cognitive styles are independent from each other, both may develop independently in the same individual. This latter possibility of simultaneous development we will describe as *bicognitive development* which will be discussed in greater detail in Chapter 7.

Another caution regarding Witkin's conceptual framework con-cerns the use of the word "dependence." It is far too easy to con-clude that field dependence means "dependent personality." In addition, the word "dependent" has come to acquire negative con-notations. For these reasons we have decided to substitute the word "sensitive" for dependent. The word "sensitivity" better describes the behavior of people with this cognitive style. It is their greater sensitivity to the social and physical environment that distinguishes them from field-independent persons on many tasks. (From this point on, field sensitive will be used in place of field dependent.)

The Relationship between Socialization Styles and Cognitive Styles

As was mentioned earlier, cross-cultural research has shown a relationship between socialization practices and cognitive style (Witkin, 1967). Interest in the relationship of socialization practices to cognitive style developed as a result of a consistent finding in most studies done in the United States: Men were more field independent and women more field sensitive. This finding led to an intensive study of socialization practices of mothers as related to the variables of field sensitivity and field independence in their sons (Dyk & Witkin, 1965). As a result of the findings of this study, a field-sensitive "socialization" cluster was identified. Socialization practices of the field-sensitive "socialization" cluster emphasized respect for social convention, protectiveness, and close ties between mother and child prior to adolescence.

Research (Witkin, 1967) on socialization styles also showed that sex differences in cognitive style result from socialization practices. Child-rearing practices used with most female children tended to be very similar to those used with field-sensitive boys. Additional factors indicating that sex differences in cognitive style were due to cultural differences as reflected in socialization practices were obtained from the results of a study by Iscoe and Carden (1961). They found that boys who were popular with their peers were more likely to be field independent, whereas popular girls were usually field sensitive. The authors conclude:

> The descriptions Witkin uses to characterize field independent versus dependent persons might well represent the kinds of behavior our *middle-class culture fosters and rewards at these ages.* Boys are expected to be somewhat aggressive, direct, and analytic, while girls

are taught a more submissive, conforming, "ladylike" type of behavior [p. 184; emphasis added].

The Iscoe and Carden study, thus, provides an introduction to examination of the relationship between culture and field sensitivity/field independence.

The discovery that sex differences in field sensitivity/independence appeared to be related to the different socialization practices used to rear male children (as contrasted with practices used to rear female children) in American society led to the hypothesis that since values of different cultures are reflected in socialization practices, people whose values differ would differ in cognitive style. This hypothesis was supported by a study comparing cognitive styles of Jewish American and Anglo–American children (Dershowitz, 1971). Dershowitz based his study partially on the assumption that the Orthodox Jewish family is one which tends to be characterized by a mother who is dominant, tending to encourage the child to form a close relationship with her, and a father who is only minimally involved in child rearing. Dershowitz reasoned that this would produce a socialization cluster more oriented toward field sensitivity. He further reasoned, not unlike Iscoe and Carden (1961), that the socialization practices of middle-class Anglo–Saxon Protestant families were more oriented to field independence. On the basis of these two assumptions, Dershowitz predicted and found that Orthodox Jewish boys scored more often in the direction of field sensitivity while Anglo–Saxon Protestant boys scored in the direction of field independence. The second phase of this study also produced some interesting results. Reasoning that the socialization cluster of the Anglo–Saxon Protestant middle class represents the dominant acculturative force in American society, he studied a third group of New York Jewish boys from families who had adopted values more characteristic of middle-class Anglo–Saxon Protestants. In line with his expectation, he found the scores of these boys to be intermediate in position—i.e., less field sensitive than the Orthodox Jewish boys, but less field independent than the Anglo boys.

Considering the characteristics of Mexican American culture in traditional communities described in Chapter 3, it could be predicted that traditional Mexican American children, like Orthodox Jewish children, would score in a more field-sensitive direction than Anglo–American children. As was mentioned earlier, the results of two studies, one in Houston, Texas, and the other in Riverside, California, confirmed this expectation. In the Houston study (Ramírez & Price–Williams, 1974a), 180 fourth graders (60 Mexican Americans, 60 Anglo–Americans, and 60 blacks) of the same socioeconomic class and religion (Catholic) were tested with the Portable Rod and Frame Test. The results are presented in Table 4.1.

In the Riverside desegregation study (Canavan, 1969), 596 Mexican American and 571 Anglo–American children in grades kindergarten through six of several schools were tested with the Man-in-the-Box Test (an instrument similar to the Portable Rod and Frame Test). The result of this study also showed that Mexican American children scored in a significantly more field-sensitive direction than Anglo–American children.

The data of the Houston and Riverside study also showed that there is considerable intragroup variability among Mexican American children. These findings and the results of the Dershowitz study led us to hypothesize that Mexican American children reared in families which had amalgamated more Anglo–American middle-class values would score more field independently than those children reared in families who were most identified with traditional Mexican American values. The next chapters discuss variables that result in intragroup variations in Mexican American culture which in turn result in variation in cognitive style among Mexican American children.

TABLE 4.1

Mean Portable Rod and Frame Test Scores of Mexican American, Anglo–American, and Black American Fourth-Grade Students

Ethnic group	Mexican Americans ($N = 60$)		Anglo–Americans ($N = 60$)		Black Americans ($N = 60$)	
	$\bar{X}$	SD	$\bar{X}$	SD	$\bar{X}$	SD
Male	14.56	7.80	6.98	5.04	14.02	7.91
Female	17.26	6.80	9.56	7.50	17.73	6.94

Summary

Research has shown that Mexican American and Anglo–American children perform differently on cognitive tasks as well as on tasks reflecting incentive–motivational and human–relational styles. These findings can be explained by the conceptual framework of field sensitivity/field independence. It was hypothesized that differences in cultural values are reflected in socialization practices, which in turn result in differences in cognitive style between Mexican American and Anglo–American children. That is, Mexican American children are relatively more field sensitive and Anglo–American children more field independent in cognitive style.

References

Beman, A. T. Piagetian theory examined cross-culturally. Unpublished doctoral dissertation, Rice University, 1972.

Canavan, D. Field dependence in children as a function of grade, sex, and ethnic group membership. Paper presented at the meeting of the American Psychological Association, Washington, D.C., 1969.

Cohen, R. A. Conceptual styles, culture conflict and nonverbal tests of intelligence. *American Anthropologist,* 1969, **71,** 828–856.

Dershowitz, A. Jewish subcultural patterns and psychological differentiation. *International Journal of Psychology,* 1971, **6**(3), 223–231.

DiStefano, J. J. Interpersonal perceptions of field independent and dependent teachers and students. Working Paper Series No. 43, London, Ontario: University of Western Ontario, Nov. 1970.

Dyk, R. B., & Witkin, H. A. Family experiences related to the development of differentiation in children. *Child Development,* 1965, **36,** 21–55.

Fitzgibbons, D., Goldberger, L., & Eagle, M. Field dependence and memory for incidental material. *Perceptual and Motor Skills,* 1965, **21,** 743–749.

Gazzaniga, M. S., & Sperry, R. W. Simultaneous double discrimination responses following brain bisection. *Psychonomic Science,* 1966, **4**(7), 261–262.

Gazzaniga, M. S., & Young. In TenHouten, W. D., Cognitive styles and social order. Final Report, Part II. O.E.O. Study Nonr. B00-5135, "Thought, race, and opportunity." Los Ángeles: University of California, 1971. P. 22.

Iscoe, I., & Carden, J. A. Field dependence, manifest anxiety and sociometric status in children. *Journal of Consulting Psychology,* 1961, **25**(2), 184.

Kagan, S., & Madsen, M. C. Cooperation and competition of Mexican, Mexican American and Anglo American children of two ages under four instructional sets. *Developmental Psychology,* 1971, **5,** 32–39.

Konstadt, M., & Forman, E. Field dependence and external directedness. *Journal of Personality and Social Psychology,* 1965, **1**(5), 490–493.

Lesser, G. S., Fifer, G., & Clark, D. H. Mental abilities of children from different social class and cultural groups. *Monographs of the Society for Research in Child Development.* 1965, **30**(4, Whole No. 102).

McClelland, D. C., Atkinson, J. W., Clark, R. A., & Lowell, E. L. *The achievement motive.* New York: Appleton, 1953.

Messick, S. The criterion problem in the evaluation of instruction: Assessing possible, not just intended outcomes. In M. C. Wittroch, & D. E. Wiley (Eds.), *The evaluation of instruction: Issues and problems.* New York: Holt, 1970.

Messick, S., & Damarin, F. Cognitive styles and memory for faces. *Journal of Abnormal and Social Psychology,* 1964, **69**(3), 313–318.

Oltman, P. K. A portable rod-and-frame apparatus. *Perceptual and Motor Skills,* 1968, **26**(2), 503–506.

Ornstein, R. E. Right and left thinking. *Psychology Today,* 1973, **6**(12), 86–92.

Pollak, I. W., & Kiev, A. Spatial orientation and psychotherapy: An experimental study of perception. *Journal of Nervous and Mental Disease,* 1963, **137**(1), 93–97.

Ramírez III, M. Cognitive styles and cultural democracy in education. *Social Science Quarterly,* 1973, **53,** 895–904.

Ramírez III, M., & Price–Williams, D. R. The relationship of culture to educational attainment. Center for Research in Social Change and Economic Development, Rice University, 1971.

Ramírez III, M., & Price–Williams, D. R. Cognitive styles of children of three ethnic groups in the United States. *Journal of Cross-Cultural Psychology*, 1974a, **5** (2).

Ramírez III, M., & Price–Williams, D. R. Values, socialization practices and attitudes toward education in mothers of three ethnic groups in the United States. Unpublished manuscript, 1974b.

Ramírez III, M., & Price–Williams, D. R. Achievement motivation in Mexican American children. Unpublished manuscript, 1974c.

Ramírez III, M., & Price–Williams, D. R. Affiliation, succorance, and nurturance in children of three ethnic groups in the United States. Unpublished manuscript, 1974d.

Ruble, D. N., & Nakamura, C. Y. Task orientation versus social orientation in young children and their attention to relevant social cues. *Child Development*, 1972, **43**, 471–480.

Stodolsky, S. S., & Lesser, G. S. Learning patterns in the disadvantaged. *Harvard Educational Review*, 1967, **37**(4), 546–593.

TenHouten, W. D. Cognitive styles and social order. Final Report, Part II. O.E.O. Study Nonr B00-5135, "Thought, race, and opportunity." Los Angeles, California: University of California, July 1971.

Witkin, H. A. Psychological differentiation and forms of pathology. *Journal of Abnormal Psychology*, 1965, **70**(5), 317–336.

Witkin, H. A. A cognitive style approach to cross-cultural research. *International Journal of Psychology*, 1967, **2**(4), 233–250.

Witkin, H. A., Dyk, R. B., Faterson, H. F., Goodenough, D. R., & Karp, S. A. *Psychological differentiation.* New York: Wiley, 1962.

5

Intracultural Variability, Socialization Practices, and Cognitive Styles

Introduction

In three Southern California communities, Mexican American children and their mothers were tested using the measures listed in Table 5.1 (Ramírez, Castañeda, & Herold, 1974). The communities differ in the degree to which their Mexican American residents identify with the values of traditional Mexican American culture that were described in Chapter 3. The subjects selected for the research were first-, fourth-, and sixth-grade children and their mothers. Both parents of each child are Mexican American and have lived in the United States over 5 years.

The first community has many characteristics in common with those of the traditional community. Most of its residents are of Mexican descent; Spanish is the primary language of most residents; most residents are closely identified with the tenets of Mexican

TABLE 5.1

Means of All Dependent Variables for the Three Mexican American Communities

Measures	A traditional community $N = 137$		A dualistic community $N = 170$		An atraditional community $N = 234$	
	$\bar{X}$	SD	$\bar{X}$	SD	$\bar{X}$	SD
PRFT (children)	17.18	6.96	14.69	7.65	13.26	7.60
DAPT (mothers)	2.56	1.28	2.26	1.10	2.06	1.65
Socialization questionnaire	14.01	3.47	12.43	3.24	7.62	4.96
Family-values questionnaire	13.05	2.20	12.92	2.47	8.81	5.34

Catholic ideology; there are close ties between most families in the community; and there is strong identification with Mexican and Mexican American heritage.

The second community, on the other hand, includes a number of Anglo–American residents. English is the primary language of most Mexican Americans in this community, and approximately 20% of these families are Protestant.

The third community is urban, located near the civic center of one of the largest cities in the Southwest. Although most of the residents of this community are Mexican American, they have more daily contact with Anglo–Americans—in school, employment, and recreation—than the residents of the other two communities. English is the primary language of the majority of Mexican Americans in this community, and more than 30% of these families are Protestant. Roles within the family are undergoing rapid change, possibly due in large part to the fact that in many families both the mother and the father are employed outside the home.

To determine cognitive style, children were tested with the Portable Rod and Frame Test (PRFT) and their mothers were given the Draw-A-Person Test (DAPT). To determine degree of identification with traditional Mexican American culture, mothers completed a socialization questionnaire and a Mexican American family-values questionnaire.

In the first community, where the socialization questionnaire and the family-values instrument showed greater agreement with "traditional" Mexican American values, children and mothers scored in a field-sensitive direction. Scores in the third community, that most unlike the traditional, were in a more field-independent direction, while scores in the second community were in between. These results indicate the importance of considering how intracultural variability affects development of cognitive styles in Mexican American children. Sources and factors contributing to diversity in Mexican American culture and the effect of diversity on the development of cognitive style in Mexican American children will be the topic of this chapter.

There is diversity not only in the regions of Mexico from which people migrate to the United States, but also in the forces that affect values and changes in values in the different environments of the United States where Mexican Americans live. In large urban centers, for the most part, Mexican Americans do not control community social, economic, and political institutions, and, therefore, are often helpless in the face of discrimination. This situation has led many Mexican American parents to conclude that it is best to socialize their children in a manner which will result in relative conformity to the mainstream American middle class, or, rather, to their conception of it, hoping that this will ensure social acceptance for these children. The situation is much different in the smaller communities of the Rio Grande Valley of Texas, or New Mexico, where Mexican Americans comprise the majority of the population and where discrimination is either nonexistent or less intense. In these areas, parents encourage their children to learn Spanish and to identify with Mexican and Mexican American history and culture.

In our research with Mexican Americans in different communities in the Southwest, we have identified the following variables which contribute to most of the diversity observed.

1. Distance from the Mexican border.   In general, the more distant a Mexican American community is from Mexico, the more likely are its members to have incorporated values of the mainstream American middle class. Proximity to Mexico facilitates communication with Mexican relatives and friends and thus reinforces identification with traditional Mexican American values.

2. Length of residence in the United States. The longer members of a community have been living in the United States the more likely it is that they have incorporated values of the majority culture. The exceptions to this are communities which are either very close to the Mexican border or which have been relatively isolated from American urban environments. Examples of these exceptions are the Rio Grande Valley of Texas and northern New Mexico.

3. Identification with Mexican, Mexican American, or Spanish American history. Mexican Americans in communities in which there is considerable identification with Hispanic history have incorporated fewer of the mainstream United States values than those in communities which lack this identification. Ethnic pride reinforces the maintenance of the traditional Mexican American system of values.

4. Degree of American urbanization. Mexican Americans residing in urban communities have incorporated more values of the mainstream American middle class than those residing in nonurban areas. Exceptions to this are communities close to the Mexican border where exposure to Mexican urbanization may be greater than to American urbanization. For example, residents of San Antonio, Texas, may be influenced more by Monterrey, Mexico, which they visit often, than by American cities.

5. Degree of economic and political strength of Mexican Americans in the community. Mexican Americans are more likely to remain identified with the traditional Mexican American value system in communities where they own businesses and participate actively in politics. In these communities, Mexican Americans serve as success models and there is less need to incorporate mainstream American values in order to achieve economic and academic success.

6. Degree of prejudice. In communities where Mexican Americans are subjected to much discrimination, members are more likely to incorporate mainstream American values. Mexican Americans in these communities often conclude that the only avenue to acceptance by the majority culture is to reject their own ethnic identity.

7. Degree of contact with non-Mexican Americans. The more a community facilitates contact between Mexican Americans and other cultures, the more likely it is that Mexican Americans will incorporate new or different values. Intermarriage between Mexican Americans and Anglo–Americans is also more likely in these communities.

These seven variables contribute in varying degrees to contemporary changes and characteristics of Mexican American communities. Based on our research on the relationships of socialization practices and community characteristics to development of cognitive styles in children, we devised a classification system for Mexican American communities. Obviously, this classification does not hold for all communities; nonetheless, we found that most Mexican American communities we studied could be classified effectively as traditional, dualistic, or atraditional. We also found that the majority of residents in traditional communities tended to be field sensitive in cognitive style, whereas those of atraditional communities were predominantly field independent (Ramírez *et al.*, 1974).

Characteristics of Mexican American Communities

Traditional Mexican American Communities

The development of values of Mexican Americans living in traditional communities is more affected by Mexican culture than by majority American culture. Values of most members of these communities are very similar to those identified in Chapter 3 as "traditional."

Most of these communities are rural, located near the Mexican border, with close cultural ties with Mexico. Mexican Americans usually comprise a majority of the population of traditional communities and consequently have considerable political and economic power. Most traditional communities are located in southern Texas, in border areas of New Mexico, and in the San Joaquin and Coachella Valleys and border areas of California.

Dualistic Mexican American Communities

Mexican Americans of dualistic communities feel pressure to incorporate values of the mainstream American middle class. How-

ever, this is counterbalanced by similar pressures to maintain identification with traditional Mexican values. (There are also pressures
to incorporate values of other ethnic groups that reside in these communities.) In general, the "more middle-class" Mexican Americans
living in these communities have incorporated more of the majority
American values.

Mexican Americans are a minority and usually have only minimal
economic or political influence. Dualistic communities are generally
semiurban and located farther from the Mexican border than traditional communities. Dualistic communities are found in or near large
cities of the Southwest, in the greater Los Angeles metropolitan area
(examples are Riverside and San Bernardino) and in the San Francisco Bay area (San Jose).

Atraditional Mexican American Communities

In atraditional communities, Mexican Americans are subject to intense pressures to incorporate values of the mainstream American
middle class. The atraditional community is usually urban or suburban and distant from Mexico. Mexican Americans are a minority in
atraditional communities and experience continual contact with
Anglo–Americans. Atraditional communities are found in the Los
Angeles metropolitan area (sections of eastern Los Angeles such
as Montebello, Monterey Park, and Whittier) and also in suburban
areas of other cities of the Southwest.

Characteristics of Communities:
Mexican American Socialization Practices

We have found that in general the differences among Mexican
American communities described previously affect values and
socialization practices—resulting in differences in cognitive-style
development. Some of these value and cognitive-style differences
will be discussed in terms of these three community types.

However, it should be emphasized once again that the classifica-
tions, *traditional, dualistic,* and *atraditional,* are not absolute. Some

communities do not fall easily into one particular category; likewise, not all Mexican American residents of the same community hold values exactly as we have outlined. Within any given community, some degree of variability will be observed from individual to individual. Yet, the values discussed are those most often observed in these community settings, and are consequently useful for analysis of cognitive styles. (See also Chapter 3, p. 40.)

Traditional Community

Identification with Family, Community, and Ethnic Group

The traditional community is a cohesive unit. There are close ties between most families which are often related by blood, marriage, or religious ceremony. Usually the extended families of most Mexican Americans in traditional communities also reside in that community, and most of the community participates in the socialization of children. Consequently, children develop strong identification with community and family.

The traditional community is ethnically homogeneous; most residents in these communities are Mexican American. Mexican and/or Mexican American history is an integral part of their lives. Most families, and often the communities themselves, have histories which are closely linked to the history of the ethnic group. Older members of the community teach the ethnic history to the younger members. The primary language spoken in traditional communities is Spanish. These factors lead to the development of a strong sense of identification with the ethnic group.

Personalization of Interpersonal Relationships

In traditional communities, relationships within the extended family take precedence over those outside the family, though these are themselves based on the family ties. An individual is encouraged to form friendships with persons with whom his own family has ties. Thus the success or failure of a relationship between two individuals affects the nature of the relationship between their respective families. Proper behavior in interpersonal relationships, then, is emphasized in child socialization. Children are socialized to establish close personal ties, to help others, and to avoid offending. Children reared in the environment of traditional communities also develop sensitivity to social cues.

They are also socialized to "achieve cooperatively" and to achieve "for the family." This reinforces the cohesiveness and integrity of the family, the community, and the ethnic group.

Status and Role Definition in Family and Community
The main goals of child socialization in the traditional community are embodied in two words: *respeto* (respect) and *bien educado* (well-educated socially). The child is socialized to respect the status of others in his family and in the community and to fulfill the responsibilities of his assigned role. Status and roles in the community and family are determined by age and sex. Older people are accorded greater status; older children are given more responsibility; tasks are assigned on the basis of sex. A clearly defined hierarchy of authority within the family ascribes to the father and mother the greatest degree of authority, followed by the oldest child. Early in life, children are encouraged to emulate the behavior of adults, especially parents, older siblings, and other relatives. The child who behaves like an adult is considered *bien educado* and contributes to the status of his parents.

Mexican Catholic Ideology
Mexican Catholic ideology emphasizes respect for convention. Specifically, it emphasizes self-control, for many emotions and behaviors of children are viewed as potentially selfish and antisocial (and thus potentially sinful). The goals are adherence to rules of the family, community, and ethnic group; suppression of rebelliousness, and subordination of individual needs and interests to those of family, community, and ethnic group.

Mexican Catholic ideology also warns of the constant threat of sin. The world outside the family, community, and ethnic group is seen as potentially dangerous and may lead children into sin unless they are properly guided by adults. Guilt is also an important aspect of Mexican Catholic ideology in child socialization. If children rebel against convention or do not perform in accordance with the expectations of their parents or other important adults, their actions are considered a transgression against God.

Cognitive Style
Emphasis on respect for family and religious authority and the emphasis on group identification results in development of a field-sensitive cognitive style in most children reared in traditional communities.

Summary
Children socialized in traditional communities (1) develop strong identification with the family, community, and ethnic group; (2) establish close personal ties to others; (3) achieve cooperatively; (4) develop sensitivity to social stimuli; (5) demonstrate respect for others; (6) respect convention; (7) exercise self-control; (8) emulate parents and other adults; and (9) are usually field sensitive in cognitive style.

Below is an excerpt from an interview with a college student who was reared in a traditional community:

Most of the families in my town in South Texas came there together from Mexico and are related to each other. The population of the town is about 98% Mexican American. Everyone speaks Spanish all the time, except at school in our classes. Even the signals in the football huddles were called in Spanish.

We used to hear lots of stories from the older people about the history of our town and the people there. The older people told stories about how steamships used to come up the Rio Grande and also about the revolution in Mexico. Some of our grandparents would tell stories about when they served in Villa's or Obregon's army.

One thing I remember most about when I was growing up was always being reminded that I had to behave right. My parents told me that if I did something wrong I shamed my family, and my behavior reflected on them. I was always told I should have respeto for them—my parents—and for others too, and that I must be a bien educado. "De que te sirve la educacion si no sabes como portarte entre la gente?" (A school education wasn't good enough, you had to behave well.) I was always supposed to answer "mande usted" if someone called me, and treat everyone with respect.

If I misbehaved, other people in the town made sure my parents found out about it, and my father would punish me. It was always easier to get along with my mother. She would fool around with us kids and listen to our side of things, but my father was serious and we always treated him with respect—kind of formally. He didn't kid around, except once in a while with the younger kids.

I was always told by my parents that I would have a responsibility to take care of them someday, and to help anybody related to me. Also, whenever I did something in school or sports very well, everyone seemed proud of me, not just my parents.

The other thing I remember is that it seemed as if we were always going to Church—for baptisms, funerals, processions, and confession. The priest was always lecturing us kids on respect and obedience. It wasn't just going to Church, though. The men belonged to Knights of Columbus and the women belonged to Cofradia del Sagrado Rosario. My friends and I belonged to C.Y.O. (Catholic Youth Organization) and almost everything we did was tied to the Church somehow.

In this student's recollections of his childhood experiences in a traditional community, we find three variables which are closely identified with development of field sensitivity in Mexican American children: (1) exposure to traditional Mexican American culture is indicated by the predominant use of Spanish; (2) development of group identification is illustrated by his identification with family and community; (3) there is in this account an emphasis on respect for family and religious authority.

Dualistic Community

Identification with Family, Community, and Ethnic Group

The dualistic community is less cohesive than the traditional community. Mobility, which is characteristic of families in dualistic communities, impedes the establishment of strong, lasting ties with families of any one community. Furthermore, the extended family of persons living in the dualistic community does not live in the same community, although most members live in close proximity. Child rearing is primarily the responsibility of the nuclear family, and does not include much participation by the extended family or the community. Children in dualistic communities develop strong *family* identification but weak *community* identification.

The dualistic community is ethnically heterogeneous. Mexican Americans and members of other ethnic groups usually live in the same neighborhoods. In fact, Mexican Americans are usually a minority.

Some families in the dualistic community have historical ties to the ethnic group, but usually the community itself does not. Consequently, the history of the ethnic group is less accessible, and ethnic identification is not as strong as it is in a traditional community. While Spanish is the primary language of adults, English is spoken by most children.

Personalization of Interpersonal Relationships

In the dualistic community, early childhood relationships are most strong within the family, but in adolescence, with the realization of peer relationships, the family ties weaken. Children are usually introduced into peer groups by older siblings and other relatives, and, therefore, membership in these groups parallels family ties. The peer group plays a critical role in the socialization of adolescents. Relationships in peer groups are very close, long-lasting, and demand commitment for mutual help. This demand sensitizes peer-group members to social cues in order that they be able to respond to the needs of others. Competition for status between peer groups introduces a cautious quality into children's interpersonal relationships.

Status and Role Definition in Family and Community

In the dualistic community, considerable emphasis is placed on socializing children to exhibit *respeto* and to be *bien educados,* but these goals are more difficult to achieve than in the traditional community. This is attributable to the fact that the teachings of the family are not often reinforced by the community. Moreover, the peer group tends to deemphasize the importance of these behaviors. In addition, peer models sometimes acquire more status than adult models, for adolescents feel that adults, particularly those who do not speak English, are less effective in teaching them how to cope with Anglo–American society. This is further complicated by the fact that status and roles are more difficult to define, since they are influenced by mainstream American middle-class values. In general, Anglo–American values deemphasize the importance of age in delineation of role and status.

Mexican Catholic Ideology

Values related to Mexican Catholicism have little influence on child socialization in the dualistic community. Protestant ideology and, with it, mainstream American values, has had an impact on these communities, making the ideas and practices of Mexican Catholic ideology seem outmoded and authoritarian to Mexican American youths.

More often than do peer groups of traditional communities, peer groups of dualistic communities socialize young people to question the values of their parents and institutions.

Cognitive Style

In dualistic communities, the decline in importance of authority and greater emphasis on individual identity result in the development of cognitive styles in children that are more field independent than those of children in traditional communities.

There is also more variability in cognitive styles in dualistic communities. Among the reasons for this variability are: (1) some children in dualistic communities have been reared in traditional communities at an earlier period of their lives—it is not unusual to find families in which older children grew up in traditional communities, while younger children were reared in the dualistic community; and (2) one parent may have been reared in a traditional community, and the other in a dualistic community.

Summary

In the dualistic community, children are socialized to have a strong identification with the family, but identification with the community and ethnic group is usually not as pronounced as in traditional communities. Children achieve cooperatively with members of their peer groups, but are competitive and cautious in interpersonal relationships outside their own peer groups. Peers are emulated more than adults, and self-control and adherence to convention are less important than in traditional communities. Needs and interests of the individual acquire as much importance of those of the family.

A college student reared in a dualistic community described some of his experiences as follows:

I grew up in a barrio *in San Antonio, Texas. Most of the people living around us were Chicanos, but blacks lived in the East Terrace Courts, east of us.*

We lived back of my grandmother's house. My aunts, uncles, and cousins lived in the surrounding area. It seemed like a little fort, you know, and we all lived within this compound.

I don't know when it started to separate, but I guess when I was about seven or eight. Slowly but surely we started breaking away from the compound. My mother and two of my brothers finally moved to California.

My brothers and I were very free, especially after I was in the gang. I used to leave home for three days at a time, and not even show up.

Our gang was called the East Side, We were very pushy, I guess, because it was all the East Side, and all the gang members were related just about. All my cousins were in the gang. My brother was a member before me. It was expected for me to go in there, you know.

It was true friendship for the gang. Every one of those guys would give his life for you. There was no doubt in my mind that if I ever got in trouble that the guys would never leave me and run. And I was in situations where there were only 3 of us and 12 of the other guys, and not one of the 3 ran away. We all stuck it out and fought. Our friendship was that close.

The guys still get together even now that they are married. They are still very much part of the gang. One of my cousins has established a nice house in the middle of the barrio. *He has bought prop-*

erty around there like mad, and he is doing a good business. All the old gang members of 10 or 15 years ago come and play pool at his place. They keep the flavor of the gang, but they don't roam around there any more. They are veterans.

Somebody always asks me why the gangs didn't speak traditional Spanish. In my opinion, the language of the barrio *gang has to be different from what is spoken at home. With a gang you are trying to establish a different thing for yourself, you know. Outside the family. So you have to have different words to express yourself. You have to make the language change to reflect what you are living. So a* pachuco *would say* jalar *for going to work, not* trabajo. *You say* jalar *because it is manual work. So if you belong to a gang, you just have a different language.*

This student's report of his early family life in a dualistic community indicates that identification with traditional Mexican American culture and group identification (particularly peer-group identification) figured importantly in his personality development. Respect for family and religious authority, however, appears to be deemphasized. There is also a decrease in the sense of identification with the family. The peer group took precedence over the family, even to the extent of developing a unique language, which in part served to separate the peer group from the family experience.

Atraditional Community

Identification with Family, Community, and Ethnic Group
The atraditional community is characterized by little or no ethnic cohesiveness. Ties between families are superficial and usually involve little or no commitment for mutual help. The extended family of persons living in the atraditional community lives neither in the community nor in close proximity to it. Children, then, are socialized by the nuclear family, and identify with the family but not with the community.

The atraditional community, like the dualistic community, is ethnically heterogeneous, with an Anglo–American majority. Often Mexican Americans tend to deemphasize their ethnic identity, and English is the primary language of both adults and children. Ethnic history is often completely unknown and unavailable in atraditional communities. Consequently, children have no opportunity to identify with Mexican American culture.

Personalization of Interpersonal Relationships

Peer relationships in dualistic communities are usually separated from family ties, and take precedence over family relationships very early in the child's life. In contrast to peer relationships in dualistic communities, however, these relationships in atraditional communities are usually short-lived, often due to the mobility which characterizes these families.

Children are socialized to be individually competitive in interpersonal relationships. Achievement for the *self* is emphasized more than cooperative achievement, and sensitivity to social cues is slow to develop.

Status and Role Definition in Family and Community

Respeto and becoming a *bien educado* are not important goals of child socialization in atraditional communities. Academic achievement receives primary emphasis, and achievement in the social sphere is of secondary importance.

Because of the great social pressure and change to which Mexican American families in atraditional communities are subject, and because of differences in value orientations found in the community, definition of status and roles is not consistent, and often contradictory.

Mexican Catholic Ideology

Mexican Catholicism plays little part in child socialization in atraditional communities. Consequently, respect for convention is emphasized only very early in the child's life and then only minimally. The behavior of children in preadolescence and adolescence is affected by Anglo–American youth culture, which often encourages criticism of convention. In addition, children learn to place increasing value on their own needs and interests.

Cognitive Style

Lack of emphasis on respect for religious and family authority, and the increased emphasis on individual or separate identity seen in atraditional communities result in development of cognitive styles more field independent than those of children raised in either traditional or dualistic communities.

While the cognitive style which predominates in atraditional communities is field independent, here, as in dualistic communities, there is a high degree of variability. Factors similar to those mentioned in conjunction with the dualistic communities also operate here. In addition, the greater frequency of ethnically mixed marriages increases this variability.

Summary

Children in atraditional communities are socialized to achieve an identity independent of the family, community, and ethnic group. Their interpersonal relationships are competitive and academic achievement is more highly valued than are social skills. Children are more likely to criticize social conventions and give more attention to their needs and interests.

The following is an excerpt from an interview with a college student reared in an atraditional community.

I was born in Detroit. Then we lived in Allen Park, a suburb of Detroit. Allen Park is mostly Anglo. There are also some Polish, Irish, and Italians living there. We knew three other Chicano families who lived there. My brothers and sisters and I didn't speak any Spanish although my parents could speak it. I didn't learn much Spanish at all until I took it in high school. My younger brothers and sisters learned even less than I did.

I remember when I was going to grade school, we watched Walt Disney's Davy Crockett at the Alamo. It was a two-part television show and during the week in between parts one of my friends asked me which side I was on—the Mexicans or Davy Crockett. I said Davy Crockett. Not that I was trying not to be Mexican, but you want to identify with the hero. They sure weren't portraying the Mexicans very well, and I made that decision.

*My parents didn't know too much about Mexican culture—or at
least they didn't tell us about it. I knew our heritage was different,
but it didn't make that much difference, I guess, to me or to my
friends.*

*We moved to California when I was in high school. In school here
the Chicanos were on one side and the Anglos on another. The
Chicanos I couldn't talk to because they usually spoke Spanish except in class, and the Anglos I talked to weren't used to having
someone like me for a friend. But, finally I ended up being their
friend. The Anglos were the ones I got to know.*

*Later in college I was able to become friends with the Chicano
students probably because college atmosphere is so much different.
My Chicano friends would tease me for being a "coconut" because
of my being Anglicized, but it wasn't my fault or my parents' fault
either—they were just trying to do the best they knew.*

This student's childhood experiences illustrate a much reduced
role of traditional Mexican American culture (indicated by the fact
that learning Spanish and the history of the ethnic group were not
emphasized) and decreased group identification (certainly with respect to community and ethnic group). This report also indicates
that exposure to other ethnic groups is more common in these communities than in traditional and dualistic communities. Greater exposure to the mainstream community resulted in a difficult choice situation for this student (similar to that described in Chapter 2), as did
the ethnic separation in high school.

Summary

Variables contributing to diversity among Mexican Americans are:
distance from the Mexican border, length of residence in the United
States, identification with Mexican, Mexican American, or Spanish
American history, degree of American urbanization, degree of economic and political strength of Mexican Americans in the community,
degree of prejudice, and degree of contact with members of other
ethnic groups—including the mainstream Anglo–American. These
variables have led to the description of three types of Mexican

TABLE 5.2

A Summary of Characteristics of Traditional, Dualistic, and Atraditional Communities

Type of community	General characteristics of community	Identification with family, community, and ethnic group	Personalization of interpersonal relationships	Status and role definition	Religious ideology	Preferred cognitive style
Traditional	Small, rural, and close to the border. Most residents are Mexican Americans and usually have considerable political and economic power. Most members of the community are related to each other and their primary language is Spanish.	Strong identification with family, community, and ethnic group. Members of extended family participate in child rearing.	Relationships are close with an understood commitment for mutual help and cooperation. Most peer-groups relations are determined by family ties.	Status and roles are well-defined and based on age and sex. Socialization emphasizes *respeto*, being *bien educado*, and emulation of adult behavior.	Emphasizes self-control, self-denial, and respect for convention. Sin and guilt are dominant themes.	Predominantly field sensitive.

Dualistic	Semiurban and removed from the border. The community is ethnically heterogeneous. Moderately strong ties exist between Mexican American families in the community. The primary language of adults is usually Spanish while the primary language of children is usually English.	Strong identification with family and peer group but weak community and ethnic group ties. Child rearing is done primarily by nuclear family.	Peer-group relationships are very important and close, implying commitment for mutual help and cooperation. Many peer-group relationships are determined by family ties.	Status and roles are less clearly defined. Peer models may have more status than adult models.	Moderate emphasis on respect for convention and self-denial. Mexican Catholic ideology influenced by American Catholic ideology.	Mixed, but more in the direction of field independence.
Atraditional	Urban and distant from the border. Mexican Americans comprise a minority. Few ties between families in the community. English is the primary language of most Mexican Americans.	Identification with community and ethnic group is weak. Peer-group influences are an important part of child rearing.	Family ties have little or no influence on the establishment of interpersonal relationships.	Status and roles are more difficult to define. Peer models are usually more important than adult models.	Greater influence of Protestantism and American Catholicism.	Predominantly field independent.

American communities as they differ in the extent of identification with traditional Mexican American values: traditional, dualistic, and atraditional. Since there are some similarities between the traditional Mexican American values and the field-sensitive socialization cluster, children reared in traditional communities are likely to be field sensitive and children reared in atraditional communities field independent in cognitive style. The study of children and their mothers in three communities in Southern California is an example of this. A summary of the discussion of the characteristics of traditional, dualistic, atraditional communities is presented in Table 5.2.

References

Ramírez III, M., Castañeda, A., & Herold, P. L. Acculturation and cognitive style in three Mexican American communities. Unpublished manuscript, 1974.

6

Culturally Democratic
Educational Environments:
Language, Heritage, and Values

Introduction

"It's fine to talk about the need for including Hispanic culture and Spanish in the school, but aren't you ignoring the most important thing? Will the kids do well on academic achievement tests? Will they learn those skills which they need to survive in this society?" We are often asked these questions when we talk to school personnel about the importance of cultural aspects of culturally democratic educational environments. Our answer is that improved academic achievement in Mexican American children has been shown to result from enhancing self-esteem through inclusion of Hispanic culture and Spanish in the curriculum. Research carried out in a bicultural/bilingual program in a dualistic community, where self-esteem in Mexican American children was enhanced by emphasizing the importance of Spanish and by acquainting children with Mexican and Mexican American heritage, showed that the children who participated in the program achieved significantly higher scores on standardized achievement tests than children in control classrooms (Ramírez, Cox, & Herold, 1972).

Other research suggests that bilingual instruction results in greater achievement in mathematics for Mexican American children. In a program implemented in a border community in Texas (Anderson & Boyer, 1970) children learned math in both English and Spanish. Comparison was made with achievement of children at the same level the year before, when math was taught only in English. The total amount of time allotted to math was constant. Test results showed that children taught bilingually did better than those taught in English only.

In addition to enhanced self-esteem and academic achievement, culturally democratic educational environments strive to promote intercultural understanding between Mexican American and non-Mexican American children, teaching personnel, and parents. Also, the development of a bicultural identity in Mexican American children is considered to be one of the most important goals of culturally democratic educational environments.

In this chapter we will discuss these four goals—enhanced self-esteem, improved academic achievement, intercultural understanding, and bicultural identity—as they may be achieved through two educational components: (1) language and heritage, and (2) values.

Table 6.1 (which is an extension of Table 2.1) compares aspects of culturally democratic educational environments with the policies and practices of many of our schools regarding Mexican American children. To achieve the goals of cultural democracy in education, emphasis must be placed on changing these policies and practices so that they are consonant with the sociocultural experience and psychodynamics of the child. By incorporating the child's language, culture, values, modes of communication, motivation, relating to others, and preferred learning style into the materials, policies, and practices of the schools, these changes can be accomplished.

Some of the necessary procedures for developing culturally democratic educational environments are discussed in this chapter, emphasizing the cultural domain of educational change.

TABLE 6.1

Culturally Democratic Educational Environments and Current Educational Practices: A Comparison

	Majority of existing educational environments	Culturally democratic educational environments
Mexican American culture	Viewed as inferior and damaging, thus: 1. Children are not permitted to speak Spanish 2. Mexican and Mexican American heritage is not included in the curriculum 3. Teachers are not given instruction on values of Mexican American culture	Viewed as a valuable resource which should be reinforced and developed further through: 1. Bilingual education 2. Inclusion of Mexican and Mexican American heritage in the curriculum 3. Acquainting teachers with Mexican American cultural values
Socialization styles	Seen as interfering with child's development and, thus, Mexican American parents are not encouraged to participate in the educational process	Seen as valuable teaching styles which must be used as a basis for developing teacher training materials such as Culture Matching Teaching Strategies Parents are actively involved in educational process; community culture and school culture are integrated
Personality characteristics of children	Seen as deviant and unacceptable, thus many children are tracked or placed in classes for the educationally handicapped or educable mentally retarded	Seen as a reflection of child's learning style, human-relational style, incentive-motivational style, and communication style, and, thus, is the basis on which culturally democratic educational environments must be developed

TABLE 6.1 *(Continued)*

	Majority of existing educational environments	Culturally democratic educational environments
What is changed and how?	The child is encouraged to behave in accordance with values and life styles of school culture through pressure from the school and community, through monocultural teaching strategies, curriculum, and assessment	The educational system is changed through: 1. New teaching strategies and curriculum 2. Parent involvement 3. New assessment practices
Results	1. Low self-esteem in Mexican American children 2. Negative view of Hispanic culture and language by non-Mexican American children 3. Suspicion and conflict between Mexican American and non-Mexican American children, school personnel and parents	1. Bicultural identity in Mexican American children 2. Self-esteem in Mexican American children 3. Intercultural understanding between Mexican Americans and non-Mexican Americans 4. Higher academic achievement

Language and Heritage

Language

Attitude toward Language

The "Spanish detention slip" reproduced in Chapter 2 is a not uncommon example of the way many schools seek to discourage Mexican American children from speaking Spanish (see also United States Commission on Civil Rights, Mexican American Education Study, Report III, 1972). As indicated by Table 6.1 this practice emanated from the belief that Mexican American culture is inferior and damaging, i.e., that it interferes with intellectual and emotional development. Efforts by schools to prohibit the use of Spanish, together with the negative stereotypes of Mexicans and Mexican Americans which exist in American society, have led some Mexican American and many non-Mexican American children to remark that Spanish is a "dumb" language. It has also resulted in the initial reluctance of many Mexican American children to use Spanish in bilingual programs.

Peal and Lambert (1962) found that

> . . . the attitude an individual holds toward the other language community plays a vitally important role in his learning the other group's language in school. . . . If he views the other community with favor, he is more likely to do well in his attempts to learn the language, and vice versa [p. 19–20].

The manner in which institutions conduct their bilingual programs will have a significant effect on these views. Referring to this point, Ulibarri (1971) asks

> How is the child's native language used? How is it treated in the classroom? Is the teacher-aid the only one using it? How can a language have prestige if the professionals use only a chosen one? Can bilingual education instill pride in these youngsters? How is the second language presented? Does it get more attention or less than the native one? Does it enjoy equal prestige [p. 380]?

In the same vein she goes on to state that bilingual education will not be successful unless it is reflected in the total *ambiente* (environment) of the school.

> The program cannot be confined to the four walls of one classroom. It cannot be an isolated project. As children step out into the corridor, they are met with the school compliance *ambiente*. It must be the same as that which exists in the classroom or all is lost. The program's influence must extend beyond the classroom. All adults, both teachers and administrators, should exhibit the cultural plurality that they teach [p. 385].

Attitudes of parents toward Spanish should also be considered. Mexican American parents who are influenced by the Anglo conformity view of acculturation oppose bilingual education on the grounds that learning Spanish interferes with the ability to learn English. It is obvious, then, that if bilingual programs are to succeed, misconceptions like these must be overcome.

The institution should also concern itself with the Mexican American child's attitude toward English. As shown previously, some Mexican American children have felt ostracized by the "system" and have rebelled against it. These children may feel that learning English is being disloyal to the Mexican American group. In some cases, children are forced to choose between development of competency in English, or acceptance by the peer group. It is, therefore, not unusual for children to develop a negative attitude toward English. These negative attitudes are intensified by the eagerness of school personnel to correct a Mexican American child's English pronunciation. Such corrections are frequently accompanied by laughter and ridicule from other children in the classroom (Gumperz, 1971). All too soon, Mexican American children become fearful of speaking out in class, and even of writing in English. This atmosphere is certainly not conducive to developing positive attitudes toward a language or language community.

It becomes clear that creating positive attitudes toward the Anglo–American and Hispanic cultures and the English and Spanish languages should be an integral part of a bilingual program. The attitudinal variable is an important one to consider in evaluating the effectiveness of bilingual programs. The "total *ambiente*" of the school determines the success or failure of the bilingual program. A bilingual program cannot be simply adjoined to a culturally undemocratic educational environment: It needs the full support and active participation of the school and of the parents for it to succeed.

Language in the Classroom

If children are to develop positive attitudes toward both the Spanish and English languages, bilingual programs must give equal emphasis to both; one or the other must *not* be relegated to a secondary role. Most bilingual programs must have both English as a Second Language (ESL) and Spanish as a Second Language (SSL) programs. The English as a Second Language program permits children whose primary language is Spanish to master English without fear of ridicule; the Spanish as a Second Language program teaches Spanish to children whose primary language is English.

The characteristics of the particular community in which a language program is being implemented must be considered in the development and establishment of that program. Bilingual programs developed for communities in which Spanish is the dominant language obviously require more emphasis on English as a Second Language instruction. In addition, these programs may also require curriculum designed to help children develop a more positive attitude toward the English language. The reverse is the case for communities (dualistic or atraditional) in which most Mexican American and non-Mexican Americans do not speak Spanish fluently. These would require programs emphasizing Spanish as a second language and curriculum units that promote positive attitudes toward the Spanish language. (See Table 6.2.)

Regardless of the sociocultural characteristics of the community, equal status, value, and importance for both languages must be ensured: The teaching of Spanish must be done by teachers as well as by paraprofessionals. Well-intentioned programs utilizing and relying on the bilingual skills of paraprofessionals may unwittingly influence children's attitudes by not requiring the teacher to use both languages. [This may require provision of a Spanish as a Second Language for Teachers program (Ramírez et al., 1972). Teachers whose primary language is English will develop more proficiency in Spanish and more willingness to use Spanish in the classroom.]

Heritage

Attitude toward Heritage

Research (Madsen, 1964; Ramírez, 1970) has shown that some Mexican Americans reject their identity with Mexican American culture (see also Chapter 1, pp. 15–17 and Chapter 4, p. 40). Interviews we have conducted with Mexican American children indicate that their experiences in school lead them to conclude that in order to be academically successful they must disavow Mexican American culture. Table 6.1 shows that many schools have not included Mexican and Mexican American heritage materials in their curricula and that Mexican American children are encouraged to behave in accordance with the values and life styles of the school culture.

TABLE 6.2

Community Characteristics

	Traditional	Dualistic	Atraditional
Dominant language	Spanish	Most children speak a combination of English and Spanish	English
Attitude toward culture	Positive attitude toward Hispanic cultures	Attitudes are more often positive toward mainstream American culture than toward Hispanic cultures	Positive attitude toward mainstream American culture
Emphasis of support programs	ESL	Both ESL and SSL	SSL
Curriculum: Self-esteem, bicultural identity, and respect for cultural differences scale	Need to improve attitudes toward the English language and mainstream American culture	Need to improve attitudes toward language and culture is determined by individual child's needs	Need to improve attitudes toward the Spanish language and Hispanic cultures

This has been well substantiated by the findings of the Mexican American Education Study of the United States Civil Rights Commission (1971–1973).

In addition to experiences in the schools, Mexican American children have also been victims of negative stereotypes of Mexicans and Mexican Americans which are promoted by the mass media (Martínez, 1973). Given this situation statements such as that made by the college student who was reared in an atraditional community (see Chapter 5, pp. 98–99) are not unusual. Mexican American children are led to conclude that their heritage is something to be ashamed of and the effect is lowered self-esteem (Peterson & Ramírez, 1971).

Self-Esteem through Appreciation of Heritage

Heritage curriculum, like language, is essential for improving self-esteem. In a study by Álvarez and Ramírez (1970), Mexican American children who had received lessons in Mexican and Mexican American heritage at the Crusade for Justice School in Denver, Colorado scored significantly higher on the Coopersmith Self-Esteem Inventory than a comparable group of Mexican American children in a community where heritage lessons were not available. Similarly, children participating in the bicultural/bilingual program in Cucamonga, California (Ramírez, et al., 1972), where they were exposed to Mexican, Mexican American, and mainstream American heritage materials, scored significantly higher on a measure of self-esteem at the end of the year than they had at the beginning of the year. The children also showed signs of better adjustment to school and were less frequently absent from school than children from comparable control classrooms.

In addition to major heritage units which covered Mexican and United States national holidays and prominent figures in Mexican and United States history, local community history units were also developed for the Cucamonga program. These community units dealt with contributions by Mexican Americans and non-Mexican Americans to the history of the community of Cucamonga and the surrounding area. These local history units succeeded in involving parents, who contributed information on family history and songs and dances which they had learned as children. As part of the local history units, parents were asked to come to the classroom and talk to children about their occupations. This helped to supplement the social studies curriculum. (Most Spanish studies curricula make little or no reference to the everyday lives of parents who are poor and/or culturally different.)

Involvement of Mexican American parents is particularly critical to the academic achievement of Mexican American children. Research (Ramírez, Taylor, & Petersen, 1971) has shown that stories told by Mexican American children to picture cards depicting educational situations consistently associate success in school with active parent involvement. Observations of children participating in the Cucamonga bicultural/bilingual program indicate that this is, indeed, the case.

It is important to involve all parents in culturally democratic educational environments. Parents, Mexican American and non-Mexican American, represent the "community culture," the effective sociocultural system that the child experiences daily. Seeing Mexican American and non-Mexican American parents actively participating in the school increases the self-esteem of Mexican American children because they see acceptance of the living representation of those values that are part of their psychodynamics. They see that the adults who have been their preschool models are valued by the school. In addition, academic achievement is enhanced because there is more exposure to adults and thus more opportunity for forming those close personal relationships with adults that contribute to higher academic achievement in Mexican Americans.

Involvement of parents from the community promotes intercultural understanding: Mexican American children have an opportunity to learn more about people from other cultural backgrounds in an atmosphere of acceptance. Parent participation in the program enhances intercultural understanding among the adults. Active participation in program committees, as well as in the classroom, by Mexican American and non-Mexican American parents helps eliminate suspicion and misunderstanding. Parent Advisory Committees, PTAs, and social activities can be instrumental in achieving cooperative work experiences. As parents and teachers become involved in personnel, curriculum, budgets, and social activities committees, they learn to appreciate the backgrounds of those around them; working together toward educational improvement, they make valuable contributions to the program. Finally, the setting is conducive to development of a bicultural identity: The child is given an opportunity to identify with adults who represent his own cultural background as well as those who represent other cultures in his community.

Values

Table 6.1 indicates that most existing teacher training programs do not provide adequate information about values of Mexican American culture. Teachers' lack of preparation in this area has resulted in misunderstandings, suspicion, and conflict. Conflicts due to value differences have been very common in schools and have had negative consequences for both Mexican American and non-Mexican American children. Mexican American students have developed negative feelings toward the school and school personnel (Ramírez, et al., 1971). Non-Mexican American students, on the other hand, have become alienated from their Mexican American peers and Mexican American culture, thereby being unable to take advantage of the opportunity to learn Spanish and to become familiar with Hispanic culture. They are missing an opportunity that could help them appreciate and share more fully in the cultural richness of the Southwest.

Conflicts occurring between teachers and Mexican American students frequently prevent the establishment of a personal, informal relationship which research has shown to be essential to the success of Mexican American children in school.

The following are examples of value conflicts and misunderstandings which we have observed most frequently in the schools.

Value Conflicts

Communication Styles

Many Mexican American children prefer to communicate with one another in Spanish. For traditional Mexican Americans, speaking Spanish is often an indication of pride in being of Mexican descent. Teachers and non-Mexican American students, however, have often interpreted this behavior as rudeness. Occasionally, those who do not understand Spanish will mistakenly conclude that they are being purposely excluded from the conversation, or even being criticized. Moreover, English-speaking children have ridiculed those who speak Spanish for their lack of proficiency in English.

Human–Relational Styles

Research has shown that traditional Mexican Americans often prefer to establish a personal and informal relationship with authority figures. (See Chapter 4, pp. 62–63.) Teachers sometimes view this as a threat to their objectivity, which they often regard as essential to the teaching role. Teachers and students who do not understand this mode of human relations will sometimes conclude that the Mexican American student is trying to curry special favor from the teacher.

Incentive–Motivational Styles

Many traditional Mexican American children tend to perform poorly in situations that demand individual competition. (Among other factors, the culture discourages "showing up" one's peers.) Teachers and non-Mexican American students who are not familiar with this orientation interpret the Mexican American student's uneasiness in competitive situations as lack of motivation, fear of failure, or even as an indication of low intelligence.

Another common source of value conflicts in the schools is the teacher's tendency to behave toward all Mexican American children as if they were products of the same sociocultural system. For example, teachers who have successfully taught Mexican American children reared in a traditional community sometimes use the same techniques with children reared in dualistic and atraditional communities. This may result in confusion and alienation for some of the Mexican American children.

By familiarizing themselves with the sociocultural premises of Mexican American culture, teachers may be able to prevent interpersonal conflicts that result from value differences. Some materials and strategies that are useful for this endeavor are listed at the end of this chapter. It must be noted that many available materials are primarily oriented toward the sociocultural system of traditional Mexican Americans. It is recommended, therefore, that the personnel responsible for teacher training, or the teachers themselves, compare the information derived from these materials to the reality that exists in the local Mexican American community.

Analyzing Interpersonal Conflicts Resulting from Value Differences

In addition to acquainting teachers with values of Mexican American culture, we have found it helpful to ask them to analyze stories given by Mexican American students and parents to the SSPST cards (see Appendix A, p. 159) which involve themes of interpersonal conflicts arising from value differences between characters in the stories. We have found that this technique permits teachers to focus on their own values as well as those of their students and the parents of their students, making it possible for them to avoid such conflicts. The teachers, in small groups, read the stories. Then, with the help of a consultant, they attempt to determine the causes for the conflicts in the stories and how these conflicts could have been prevented. For example, the following stories were given to a group of elementary school teachers in southern California after they had attended a lecture on traditional Mexican American values and read related literature.

STORY

This is Juan. He is getting to school late one day. The teacher is already talking to the class. He sees him come in and right away asks him how come he is late to school. Juan says, "My parents had to go to Calexico to visit my uncle who is sick, so I had to stay with my brothers and sisters." His teacher says, "That's no excuse. Don't you have any sense of responsibility? How do you expect to graduate? Your parents should know better than to keep you from coming to school." Juan feels real bad and all the kids laugh at him. He thinks the teacher doesn't understand. He just gets embarrassed and runs all the way home.

The following are the comments of some teachers upon hearing this story.

DISCUSSION

Teacher 1: *The boy felt that he must help his family in a time of crisis. The teacher should have been more understanding. After all, family ties are important to Mexican Americans.*

Teacher 2: *Yes, it was responsibility to the school versus responsibility to the family. The boy was really caught between these two.*

Teacher 3: *The teacher didn't know that many Mexican American parents feel that responsibility at home is just as important as responsibility at school. Parents see themselves as responsible for seeing that children learn to carry out their home responsibilities.*

Teacher 4: *The teacher should have a meeting with the boy's parents to see if they can get each other to see that the boy no longer gets caught in the middle between their demands. Parents are likely to feel that the teacher does not think that responsibility to the family is important.*

STORY

This boy is being scolded by the teacher for speaking Spanish in the school grounds. The boy doesn't know what to do. He doesn't want to make the teacher angry, but he also knows his friends are watching him and if he doesn't stand up for his rights and for his people they will call him a traitor. The teacher tells him not to do it again, or she will send him to the principal. He continues to speak Spanish and is suspended for three days.

DISCUSSION

Teacher 1: *The student really didn't know what to do. He didn't want to disobey the teacher who he sees as the authority but at the same time he doesn't want his friends to think that he is ashamed of speaking Spanish.*

Teacher 2: *This could have happened to me. I used to think that it was bad for the Mexican American kids to speak Spanish. We used to have detention slips which we filled out and sent to the principal if a student was heard speaking Spanish at school.*

Teacher 3: *I think the teacher should have tried to handle this herself.*

Teaching Styles of Mexican American Parents

Equal in importance to helping teachers prevent interpersonal conflicts is training them to utilize knowledge of Mexican American values and culture to enhance academic achievement, intercultural understanding, self-esteem, and bicultural identity in Mexican American children. To facilitate the use of Mexican American values and culture in the classroom, we identified a set of teaching strategies now entitled the Culture-Matching Teaching Strategies (CMTS). These strategies evolved from research on the teaching styles of Mexican American parents in traditional communities, and have been used in training teachers in the Cucamonga program. (CMTS is included in Appendix D, p. 179.)

Use of these strategies helps Mexican American children of traditional communities feel more self-confident and achieve more success academically. Since they are more comfortable during those critical first weeks of school, much of the initial "culture shock" is avoided.

Improvement of self-esteem is also accomplished through CMTS: Some of the strategies emphasize use of Spanish, Mexican, and Mexican American heritage curricula in the classroom. These strategies enhance intercultural understanding by creating an atmosphere in the classroom that allows teachers and children to interact without conflict. Moreover, by allowing Mexican American children to explore other cultures and become acquainted with the school by way of their own language and culture, the CMTS assist in achieving the goal of developing a bicultural identity in these children.

To ascertain the degree to which CMTS resulted in increased bicultural identity and intercultural understanding, a behavior observation instrument that focused on three behavioral clusters was developed (see Bicultural Identity/Respect for Cultural Differences Scale on pp. 118–119). These behavioral clusters are discussed in the following.

1. Identification with Hispanic culture. This cluster refers to the degree to which the child's image of Hispanic culture and the Spanish language is positive and the degree to which he demonstrates a willingness to identify with it. Specific behaviors that are considered indicative of this behavioral cluster are: responding or attempting to respond in Spanish when addressed in Spanish; degree to which the child speaks Spanish spontaneously; willingness to role play Mexican or Mexican American characters in school heritage

CULTURALLY DEMOCRATIC LEARNING ENVIRONMENTS

FOLLOW THROUGH MODEL

A BICULTURAL/BILINGUAL APPROACH

BICULTURAL IDENTITY/RESPECT FOR CULTURAL DIFFERENCES SCALE

Identification with Hispanic Culture:		almost always	often	sometimes	rarely	never
1.	Responds or attempts to respond in Spanish when spoken to in Spanish.					
2.	Speaks Spanish spontaneously.					
3.	Shows willingness to role play Mexican or Mexican American heroes in heritage plays.					
4.	Wears clothing, brings objects from home which reflect an identification with Hispanic culture.					

(continued on following page)

Identification with "Mainstream" Culture:		almost always	often	sometimes	rarely	never
1.	Responds or attempts to respond in English when spoken to in English					
2.	Speaks English spontaneously.					
3.	Shows willingness to role play American (non-Mexican American) heroes in heritage plays.					

Respect for Cultural Differences:

1.	Seeks friendships with members of other ethnic groups.					
2.	Is interested in learning languages other than his/her primary language.					
3.	Is interested in social studies materials dealing with other ethnic groups.					
4.	Shows respect for languages and cultures of other ethnic groups (e.g. does not use derogatory names or laugh at children who speak another language and/or belong to another ethnic group).					

119

plays; and wearing articles of clothing, bringing toys to school, and eating foods that are identified with Hispanic culture.

2. Identification with mainstream culture. This cluster refers to the degree to which the child's image of mainstream culture and the English language is positive and the degree to which he demonstrates a willingness to identify with both the culture and the language. Specific behaviors include: responding or attempting to respond in English when addressed in English; degree to which English is spoken spontaneously; and willingness to role play Anglo–American figures in school heritage dramatizations.

3. Respect for cultural differences. Respect for persons and cultures of other ethnic groups is a positive consequence of culturally democratic educational environments. Ethnocentrism and denigration of cultural values, languages, and traditions different from one's own often result from a need to protect cultural identity when it is under assault by the school culture. The specific behaviors indicative of respect for cultural differences include: seeking to form friendships with members of other ethnic groups; demonstrating an interest in learning the languages of other groups; demonstrating an interest in social studies materials dealing with other groups; and showing respect for languages and cultures of other ethnic groups.

The three general categories of behavior discussed here served as the basis for the behavior observation instrument used in the Cucamonga program entitled Bicultural Identity/Respect for Cultural Differences Scale (see pp. 118–119).

Summary

In this chapter we have discussed four goals that may be achieved through the educational components of (1) language and heritage, and (2) values. These goals are enhanced self-esteem, improved academic achievement, intercultural understanding, and bicultural identity.

Another goal that is closely linked to development of bicultural identity is that of developing mental flexibility. The ultimate relationship between these goals is very well described by Peal and Lambert (1962):

> The picture that emerges of the French–English bilingual in Montreal is that of a youngster *whose wider experiences* in two cultures have given him advantages which a monolingual does not enjoy. Intellectually his experience with two language systems seems to have left him with a mental flexibility, a superiority in concept formation, and a more diversified set of mental abilities [p. 20].

In the next chapter we will focus on procedures for developing mental flexibility in children.

Resource Materials Recommended for Teacher Training Programs

Books and Monographs

1. Arciniega, Tomás. *Public education's response to the Mexican American student.* El Paso, Texas: Innovative Resources Incorporated, 1971. *Address:* Innovative Resources Incorporated, Post Office Box 26655, El Paso, Texas.

In this monograph, Dr. Tomás Arciniega, Dean of the School of Education at California State University at San Diego, presents a sociological model for the analysis of complex interrelationships between the school and the Mexican American community. This monograph is appropriate for advanced teacher training programs.

2. Carter, Thomas. *Mexican Americans in school: A history of educational neglect.* New York: College Entrance Examination Board, 1970. *Address:* College Entrance Examinations Board, Publications Order Office, Box 592, Princeton, New Jersey, 08540.

The author of this book, Dr. Thomas Carter, is Dean of the School of Education, California State University at Sacramento. This book provides an overview of factors that have contributed to the low educational attainment of Mexican Americans. Dr. Carter recommends changes that should be made in schools in order to ensure equality of educational opportunity for Mexican Americans. Recommended for all teacher training programs.

3. Castañeda, Alfredo, Ramírez III, Manuel, Cortés, Carlos E., & Barrera, Manuel (Eds.) *Mexican Americans and educational change: Symposium at the University of California, Riverside, May 21–22, 1971.* New York: Arno Press, 1974.

This is a collection of papers presented at the first major symposium on Mexican American education held at a university. The papers focus on four major areas—educational change in historical perspective, the politics of educational change, bicultural education, and bilingual education. Among the contributors are George I. Sanchez, Joan Moore, and Armando Rodriguez.

4. Diaz–Guerrero, Rogelio. *Estudios de psicologia del Mexicano.* Mexico City: Editorial F. Trillas, S. A., 1970. *Address:* Editorial F. Trillas, S. A., Avenida 5 de Mayo 43–105, Mexico 1, D.F.

Dr. Diaz–Guerrero is a psychiatrist and professor of psychology at the Universidad Nacional Autónoma de México. This book is a collection of his articles on the psychology of the Mexican. A number of the studies focus on cultural values. This book is available only in Spanish and is more appropriate for advanced teacher training programs.

5. Galarza, Ernesto. *Barrio boy.* Notre Dame, Indiana: University of Notre Dame Press, 1971. *Address:* University of Notre Dame Press, Notre Dame, Indiana 46556. (Also in paperback: Ballantine Books, New York, 1972.)

This novel is based on Dr. Galarza's childhood experiences. The initial chapters deal with his early childhood in several rural Mexican communities. The latter part of the book describes his exposure to Anglo–American culture in Sacramento, California. Of particular interest to school personnel is the description of his experiences in a school where teachers and administrators were sensitive to the cultural differences of the children. This book is recommended for all teacher training programs.

6. John, Vera P., & Horner, Vivian M. *Early childhood bilingual education.* New York: Modern Languages Association of America,

1971. *Address:* Materials Center, MLA-ACTFL, 62 Fifth Avenue, New York, New York 10011.

This book provides an overview of many of the bilingual programs that have been implemented across the country. The book can serve as a reference guide for administrators and teachers in bilingual programs. Included are discussions of teacher recruitment and training, and curriculum materials for both Mexican American and American Indian students. Also included is a discussion of testing and evaluation procedures for bilingual programs. Various language proficiency and intelligence or general ability tests are reviewed.

7. Padilla, Amado, & Ruíz, Rene. *Latino mental health: A review of literature.* Contract hour HSM 42–72–61 with the National Institute of Mental Health, Health Services and Mental Health Administration, Department of Health, Education and Welfare. *Address:* Center for Minority Group Mental Health Program National Institute of Mental Health, Parklawn Building, 5600 Fischers Lane, Rockville, Maryland, 20852.

Dr. Padilla, Assistant Professor of Psychology at the University of California at Santa Barbara, and Dr. Ruíz, Professor of Psychology at the University of Missouri, Kansas City have thoroughly reviewed the educational and psychological literature on Mexican Americans. The monograph covers intelligence testing, academic performance, discrimination, and verbal learning, as well as many other topics. Recommended for advanced teacher training programs.

8. United States Commission on Civil Rights: Mexican American Education Study. All reports available from the Superintendent of Documents, U.S. GPO, Washington, D.C. 20402.

Report I: *Ethnic Isolation of Mexican Americans in the Public Schools of the Southwest* (April 1971). This report is concerned with the ethnic isolation of Mexican Americans in the public schools and with the participation of Mexican Americans in the educational process as principals, teachers, and in other official school capacities.

Report II: *The Unfinished Education* (October 1971). This report is concerned with school holding power, reading achievement, grade repetition, overageness of the student in grade assignment, and student participation in extracurricular activities.

Report III: *The Excluded Student* (May 1972). The denial of equal opportunity by exclusionary practices for Mexican Americans is examined in this report. The report indicates that the dominance of Anglo–American values is apparent in the curricula on all educational levels; in the cultural climate which ignores or denigrates Mexican American values and the use of the Spanish language; in the exclusion of the Mexican American community from full participation in matters pertaining to school policies and practices.

Report IV: *Mexican American Education in Texas: A Function of Wealth* (August 1972). This report examines the fiscal practices of the state of Texas. State aid under the Foundation Program requires Mexican American districts to pay more than their share of Foundation costs and receive three-fifths less revenue per pupil from State and local sources than Anglo–American districts.

Report V: *Teachers and Students* (March 1973). This is a report of the results of studies in classroom interactions between teachers and Mexican American students. Findings show that Mexican Americans are being denied equal educational opportunity.

Articles and Journals

1. Jaramillo, Mari–Luci. *Cultural differences revealed through language.* The National Center for Research and Information on Equal Educational Opportunity, May 1972. *Address:* The National Center for Research and Information on Equal Educational Opportunity, Box 40, Teachers College, Columbia University, New York, New York 10027.

Dr. Mari–Luci Jaramillo is chairperson of the Department of Elementary Education at the University of New Mexico. This article examines cultural differences implied in language, its syntax and use. She illustrates a few of the differences by contrasting the way an action or idea is conveyed in English with the way it is conveyed in Spanish. Dr. Jaramillo advocates a systematic introduction to the foreign language in bilingual education. The article is appropriate for all teacher training programs.

2. *The National Elementary Principle,* November 1970, **L**(2). This is a special issue on the education of the Spanish speaking. The

authors of the articles contained are social scientists and educators. Many of the articles are appropriate for all levels of teacher training.

Films

1. "I Am Joaquin." *Address:* Centro Campesino Cultural, Post Office Box 2302, Fresno, California 93701.

This film focuses on the heritage of Mexican Americans as presented through the reading of a poem written by Rodolfo "Corky" Gonzalez. The reading is combined with a series of still pictures. Very useful for all levels of teacher training. (Color film, 22 minutes, English, $300.)

2. "How is School, Enrique?" *Address:* Aims Instructional Media Services, Inc., Post Office Box 1010, Hollywood, California 90028.

This film features home and school experiences of an urban Mexican American child. Appropriate for all levels of teacher training. (Color film, 18 minutes, English, $240.)

3. "Pancho." Produced by: United States Office of Economic Opportunity through Robert K. Sharpr Productions. *Distributed by:* United States National Audiovisual Center, National Archives and Records Service, Washington, D.C. 20408.

Shows experiences of a rural Mexican American child in a Head Start program. Recommended for all teacher training programs.

Filmstrips

1. "Educational Opportunities for Mexican Americans." Produced by the Southwest Educational Development Laboratory, Austin, Texas, supported by a grant from the United States Office of Education. *Address:* Office of Mexican American Affairs, United States Office of Education, 400 Maryland Avenue, Washington, D.C. 20202.

A series of five filmstrips covering the following topics: (1) migrant programs, (2) preschool programs, (3) bilingual education, (4) secondary education, and (5) programs designed to facilitate learning English as a second language. Although somewhat out of date, these filmstrips still provide useful information for elementary teacher training programs.

Videotapes

1. "New Approaches to Bicultural/Bilingual Education." *Address:* Bilingual Dissemination Center, 6504 Tracor Lane, Austin, Texas 78721.

A series of seven videotapes and short quizzes specifically developed for teacher training programs. The quizzes are designed for self-administration and are based on the content of the videotapes. The tapes are appropriate for all levels of teacher training. (Tapes and quizzes were developed under the direction of Alfredo Castañeda, Manuel Ramírez III, P. Leslie Herold, and Barbara Goffigon Cox.)

Elementary Curriculum Materials

1. The Culturally Democratic Learning Environments, Follow Through Model Sponsor, at the University of California, Santa Cruz, has developed bilingual/bicultural curriculum materials for grades kindergarten through three. Materials may be obtained in the areas of social studies, math, reading, science, reading in Spanish, and Spanish as a Second Language for Children. Recommended for elementary teachers.

References

Álvarez, D., & Ramírez III, M. Self-Esteem in two Chicano Communities. Unpublished manuscript, 1970.

Anderson, T., & Boyer, M. *Bilingual schooling in the United States.* Vol. I and II. Austin, Texas: Southwest Educational Laboratory, 1970.

Gumperz, J. J. *Language in social groups.* Stanford, California: Stanford Univ. Press, 1971.

Madsen, W. *Mexican Americans of south Texas.* New York: Holt, 1964.

Martínez, T. Advertising and racism: The case of the Mexican-American. In O. I. Romano-V. (Ed.), *Voices.* (2nd ed.) Berkeley, California: Quinto Sol Publications, 1973.

Peal, E., & Lambert, W. E. The relation of bilingualism to intelligence. *Psychological Monographs: General and Applied,* 1962, **76**(27, Whole No. 546).

Petersen, B., & Ramírez III, M. Real ideal self disparity in Negro and Mexican American children. *Psychology,* 1971, **8**(3), 22–28.

Ramírez III, M. Identification with Mexican family values and authoritarianism in Mexican–Americans. *Journal of Social Psychology,* 1967, **73**, 3–11.

Ramírez III, M. Identity crisis in Mexican American adolescents. In H. S. Johnson, & M. W. Hernandez (Eds.), *Educating the Mexican American.* Valley Forge, Pennsylvania: Judson Press, 1970.

Ramírez III, M., Cox, B., & Herold, P. L. Culturally Democratic Learning Environments, A Bicultural/Bilingual Approach. Follow Through Project, University of California, Riverside. Annual Report 1971–1972.

Ramírez III, M., Taylor, C., & Petersen, B. Mexican American cultural membership and adjustment to school. *Developmental Psychology,* 1971, **4**(2), 141–148.

Ulibarri, M-L. Ambiente bilingue: Professionals, parents and children. In A. Castañeda, M. Ramírez III, C. E. Cortés, & M. Barrera (Eds.), *Mexican Americans and educational change: Symposium at the University of California, Riverside, May 21–22, 1971.* New York: Arno Press, 1974.

United States Commission on Civil Rights: Mexican American Education Study, Reports I–V. 1971–1973. Superintendent of Documents, U.S. GPO, Washington, D.C.

7

Culturally Democratic
Educational Environments:
Bicognitive Development

Introduction

Most bicultural–bilingual programs and other programs attempting to develop culturally democratic educational environments have focused exclusively on language and heritage and have ignored cognitive styles. Language and heritage are critical components, yet cannot be implemented successfully in a vacuum. Concentrating efforts toward educational change in these areas exclusively, at the expense of other important considerations, will result in only superficial change at best. For example, we have visited programs implementing Hispanic heritage curricula and in which teachers present lessons in English and in Spanish, and have seen in these programs the use of teaching strategies that are inappropriate to the cognitive styles of Mexican American students. Seeds of failure and alienation exist in these environments, environments which appear superficially

129

to be conducive to success for Mexican American children. The cognitive-styles component, then, must play a central role in the development of culturally democratic educational environments.

In our research we have observed adults and children who behave in both cognitive styles—that is, they exhibit "cognitive switching"— the ability to draw upon both field-sensitive and field-independent styles at any given time. The cognitive style these individuals employ seems to be dictated by characteristics of the activity, task, or particular social atmosphere. The behavioral versatility exhibited by these persons implies to us a bicognitive development. Their behavior can reflect either cooperation or competition; they can solve problems which require inductive or deductive thought; they can respond to or effectively ignore the social environment.

The task of this component of culturally democratic educational environments is to facilitate bicognitive development in children. If children are able to utilize both the field-sensitive and field-independent cognitive styles, they will have more than one approach to apply in learning and problem solving. We believe this objective to be important for all children, regardless of cultural background. It is especially critical for Mexican American children. In order to meet the demands of two cultural environments, Mexican American children must use behaviors from both the intellectual and affective domains which are appropriate to the particular situation and the cultural environment in which it occurs. Education's efforts to help Mexican American children to function in two cultures can be facilitated by a working understanding of our concept of bicognitive development. One sociocultural system, that of traditional Mexican American communities, primarily requires the individual to respond using communication, human–relational, incentive–motivational, and learning styles of the field-sensitive mode. On the other hand, that of the mainstream American middle class usually requires field-independent behavioral responses.

The conflicts experienced by some Mexican American students can be attributed to the fact that they have not had an opportunity to learn to function in the style required by the situation. The Mexican American student experiences conflict and frustrations in his attempts to cope with the demands of either the traditional Mexican American or the mainstream American culture. This student often feels that to function successfully in one culture, he must reject the other.

This chapter focuses on a process for stimulating bicognitive development in Mexican American children. Much of this procedure evolved from research we have been doing which shows that if the cognitive style that teachers use in the classroom is matched to the cognitive style in which children learn, children's academic performance is better than that of children in control classrooms. Furthermore, the results show that if children are introduced to the unfamiliar cognitive style in terms that are consonant with their preferred style, they can begin to function effectively in *both* cognitive styles, i.e., bicognitively.

In the classrooms participating in our study, we sought to develop teaching strategies, classroom environments, curriculum, and assessment techniques and practices that are in keeping with culturally democratic educational environments as shown in Table 6.1. To accomplish this, it was necessary to do the following:

1. Assess cognitive styles in children
2. Assess cognitive styles in teachers
3. Train teachers to teach bicognitively
4. Develop curriculum and classroom environments reflecting both cognitive styles
5. Develop assessment techniques and testing environments appropriate to the cognitive styles of the children being tested

Assessing Cognitive Styles in Children

The initial step in developing educational environments that stimulate bicognitive development in children is assessment of the child's preferred cognitive style, for the child is initially instructed in his preferred style (see Figure 7.1).

Three basic difficulties are encountered in this assessment process. First, instruments which are now commercially available, such as the Portable Rod and Frame Test (PRFT), Embedded Figures Test (EFT), and the Children's Embedded Figures Test (CEFT; see Appendix B, pp. 163–165) may evaluate only the degree to which an individual is field independent. These measures probably do not indicate the

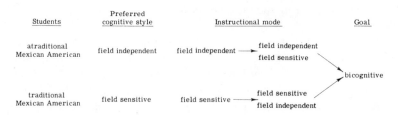

Figure 7.1. *Promoting bicognitive development in Mexican Americans.*

degree to which an individual may be field sensitive or bicognitive. (For example, some of the bicognitive children we have identified through our research have high PRFT scores, while others have scored low on this same instrument.) Second, at any one testing, the examiner using these instruments does not know if he has tapped the preferred style or merely a situationally specific response.[1] Finally, children must be periodically reexamined to determine degree of development or growth in each style.

Background Variables

As was mentioned above, one should note that all instruments now in frequent use for assessing cognitive style are specifically designed to measure field independence, not field sensitivity. These instruments give a field-independent set—it is made obvious that in order to "do well" on these tests a field-independent mode of approach must be assumed. An instrument that is less affected by situational variables imposed by the test itself and one that indicates degree of development in both styles is needed. To this end we have been doing intensive studies of Mexican American children in educational settings.

Research that we have done with field-sensitive and field-independent Mexican American children shows that the following variables relating to culture, community, and family are indicative of cognitive style.

[1] Our research shows that most people are more developed in one style or the other. The style in which they are best developed—the preferred cognitive style—is that in which they prefer to function when situational conditions do not dictate the use of the less well-developed style.

1. Socialization practices of parents. Children reared with socialization practices which emphasize respect for family, religious, and political authority are more likely to be field sensitive.

2. The characteristics of the community in which the child was reared. Children reared in traditional Mexican American communities (see Chapters 3 and 5) are more likely to be field sensitive.

3. Dominant language. Children whose primary language is Spanish are more likely to be field sensitive. Conversely, children whose primary language is English are more likely to be field independent.

4. Embeddedness in the family. A child whose ties to his family, to his mother in particular, are very strong is likely to be field sensitive. However, the child who considers himself as quite separate from other family members is more likely to be field independent (see Chapter 5).

Observable Behaviors

Our research with Mexican American children who were identified as either extremely field sensitive or field independent (as determined by the PRFT and background variables) has led to identification of school behaviors that are characteristic of these two groups of children. We have incorporated these behaviors into Field-Sensitive and Field-Independent Child Behavior Observation Instruments. These instruments reveal the degree to which a child is bicognitive, and identify his preferred style as well. The instruments can be used in a variety of situations and yield information regarding cognitive styles that is not merely situation specific. (See Appendix B for further information on use of the observation instruments.)

The school behaviors observed most frequently in field sensitive and field independent children are presented in Tables 7.1 and 7.2.

To provide a better picture of how field-sensitive and field-independent children behave in the classroom, we asked teachers to describe children whom we had identified as either extremely field-sensitive or field-independent with the child behavior observation

TABLE 7.1

Field-Independent Behaviors

Relationship to peers
1. Prefers to work independently
2. Likes to compete and gain individual recognition
3. Task oriented; is inattentive to social environment when working

Personal relationship to teacher
1. Rarely seeks physical contact with teacher
2. Formal; interactions with teacher are restricted to tasks at hand

Instructional relationship to teacher
1. Likes to try new tasks without teacher's help
2. Impatient to begin tasks; likes to finish first
3. Seeks nonsocial rewards

Characteristics of curriculum that facilitate learning
1. Details of concepts are emphasized; parts have meaning of their own
2. Deals with math and science concepts
3. Based on discovery approach

---

instruments. In no case did the teachers know how we had classified the children prior to the interview.

C. B.—FIELD-INDEPENDENT FEMALE, KINDERGARTEN

I: (Interviewer) *How would you describe C?*

T: (Teacher) *C is a very independent child. She works fine on tasks that do not require the teacher to be there. She went through a quiet period earlier in the year when her grandfather died. She isolated herself from the groups for two months, but then she worked herself in again. She can work independently without much guidance.*

I: *What are C's academic strengths?*

T: *She does fine in math. Her math is good. She had no problem with number sets. She learns concepts in math fast. In phonics, she is a little slower. She is slower remembering sounds and letters and she isn't yet to the point where she can put sounds together.*

TABLE 7.2

Field-Sensitive Behaviors

Relationship to peers
  1. Likes to work with others to achieve a common goal
  2. Likes to assist others
  3. Is sensitive to feelings and opinions of others

Personal relationship to teacher
  1. Openly expresses positive feelings for teacher
  2. Asks questions about teacher's tastes and personal experiences; seeks to become like teacher

Instructional relationship to teacher
  1. Seeks guidance and demonstration from teacher
  2. Seeks rewards which strengthen relationship with teacher
  3. Is highly motivated when working individually with teacher

Characteristics of curriculum that facilitate learning
  1. Performance objectives and global aspects of curriculum are carefully explained
  2. Concepts are presented in humanized or story format
  3. Concepts are related to personal interests and experiences of children

---

I: *How does she behave socially?*

T: *In the classroom she sort of takes a back seat to the others. She is more a follower than a leader. She doesn't really stand out from the rest of the group. You can miss her easily, if you are not conscious of the fact that she is there.*

J. C.—FIELD-INDEPENDENT MALE, KINDERGARTEN

I: *How would you describe J?*

T: *J is an only child. His father is nearly blind and cannot work anymore. His mother is more attached to J than J is to her. It seems that J has taken on the role of the man of the house. Everything J says, goes. He dominates his mother completely. He wanted to do the same with us at school but it didn't work and he spent a good deal of time feeling sorry for himself.*

I: *How does he do academically?*

T: *J has no problems academically. He picks up concepts as soon as we explain them to him and he retains a lot. Academic work doesn't present much of a challenge to him.*

I: *How does he behave socially?*

T: *He would rather be a spectator than take part in group activities. He is very aggressive and competitive. He fights to try and get his way with others. When other children bring something to show to the class, he always says that he has something better.*

He is always trying to demonstrate that he is the strongest. Recently, I started to ask him to help as part of a team. It worked; he is starting to do more things with the other kids.

E. L.—FIELD-SENSITIVE MALE, KINDERGARTEN

I: *How would you describe E?*

T: *He is very sensitive to the feelings of others and very anxious to please. He brings flowers from his grandmother's house everyday. He tries very hard to impress.*

He knows when you are not being sincere. One of the teacher's aides told me that he did an experience story for her. He knew that it wasn't very good, but he asked her what she thought of it. She told him she thought it was good and he said, "No, you don't." The aide said, "What do you mean?" He said, "I can tell it in your eyes, it isn't good, but don't lie to me."

He has been shifted around from one relative to another. At one time he lived with an aunt and uncle. He now lives with his grandmother. He is very proud of his family though. His father takes him places and he does lots of things with his father and uncles. He talks a lot about his uncles.

I: *How does he do academically?*

T: *He is very concerned about learning. He wants to make sure that I know he is learning. If I didn't call on him or if the aide didn't ask him for an answer right away he would feel hurt. If* he isn't recognized right away, he moves from his place and comes to sit next to you. He is strong in phonics. He has a tremendous memory. Phonics is his strongest subject. He really takes pride in being able to read.

I: *How does he behave socially?*

T: *E is no problem. He works very well and gets along with everyone. He is not the type to initiate fights and he does not have to prove that he is a leader.*

S. V.—FIELD-SENSITIVE FEMALE, FIRST GRADER

I: *How would you describe S?*

T: *S loves me. She is the first to arrive every morning. She loves to come and help me arrange the classroom.*

In the beginning of the year, however, she was very slow and seemed indifferent to anything that we would do in class. She was very quiet and shy. This changed when I got to know her mother and father well. The change in S came when her parents became involved in classroom activities. The change in her behavior was dramatic. She now loves to please me. She wants to know that I approve of her.

I: *How does she do academically?*

T: *She likes to do things that she can take home. It is a way that she can get praise for doing a good job.*

She is patient, she doesn't rush to get home. She prefers quality to quantity. I can tell her to do something and she will. This is quite a change from her behavior at the beginning of the year. I think the difference was that I met her parents. She felt good about the fact that I knew her parents.

Descriptions of field-sensitive and field-independent children given by their teachers and an examination of ratings obtained with the child behavior observation instruments will indicate which types of behaviors those children need to learn in order to become bicognitive. They will be able to learn these behaviors, however, only if teachers are trained to introduce the children to the unfamiliar cognitive style. To do this it is necessary to train teachers to teach bicognitively. The first step in this process is assessment of teaching style.

Assessing Cognitive Styles in Adults

Accurate assessment of cognitive styles in adults is more difficult than assessment of cognitive styles in children. Our observations show that adults are frequently more bicognitive than children, and, thus, the cognitive style they employ at any given time is more likely to be determined by situational variables. The single score obtained with instruments such as PRFT, EFT, or Draw-a-Person Test (DAPT) is less likely to indicate the degree to which each style is developed and the style that is more likely to be used in any given situation.

Unlike assessment of a child's cognitive style, assessment of a teacher's cognitive style is not as concerned with determination of the preferred style as with the situational style. That is, which style does the teacher use when she is teaching? Our observations show that this may not be the preferred style since many teachers are affected by situational variables such as content of the curriculum, school policy, or the teacher's conception of the idealized teaching role.

Observable Behaviors

Research with parents of field-sensitive children led to identification of teaching behaviors which in turn allowed us to identify teachers and paraprofessionals who taught using field-sensitive behaviors and similar strategies. We also identified several teachers and paraprofessionals who scored as very field independent on the PRFT and whose backgrounds indicated that they would be highly field independent. Intensive observation of behavior of these persons in the classrooms led to construction of the Field-Sensitive Teaching Strategies Observation Instrument and the Field-Independent Teaching Strategies Observation Instrument. The behaviors are included in Tables 7.3 and 7.4.

TABLE 7.3

Field-Independent Teaching Style

Personal behaviors
 1. Is formal in relationship with students; acts the part of an authority figure
 2. Centers attention on instructional objectives; gives social atmosphere secondary importance

Instructional behaviors
 1. Encourages independent student achievement; emphasizes the importance of individual effort
 2. Encourages competition between individual students
 3. Adopts a consultant role; teacher encourages students to seek help only when they experience difficulty
 4. Encourages learning through trial and error
 5. Encourages task orientation; focuses student attention on assigned tasks

Curriculum related behaviors
 1. Focuses on details of curriculum materials
 2. Focuses on facts and principles; teaches students how to solve problems using short cuts and novel approaches
 3. Emphasizes math and science abstractions; teacher tends to use graphs, charts, and formulas in teaching, even when presenting social studies curriculum
 4. Emphasizes inductive learning and the discovery approach; starts with isolated parts and slowly puts them together to construct rules or generalizations

---

Teacher Training

Learning to Teach in Two Cognitive Styles

Matching the teaching style of the teacher to the learning style of the children is certainly one of the reasons for assessing teaching styles in teachers, but even more important is the planning of training programs to help teachers use both field-sensitive and field-independent strategies. With the Teaching Strategies Observation Instruments, we can determine which is the unfamiliar style and which specific behaviors in this style need development or practice. With this

TABLE 7.4

Field-Sensitive Teaching Style

Personal behaviors
1. Displays physical and verbal expressions of approval and warmth
2. Uses personalized rewards which strengthen the relationship with students

Instructional behaviors
1. Expresses confidence in child's ability to succeed; is sensitive to children who are having difficulty and need help
2. Gives guidance to students; makes purpose and main principles of lesson obvious; presentation of lesson is clear with steps toward "solution" clearly delineated
3. Encourages learning through modeling; asks children to imitate
4. Encourages cooperation and development of group feeling; encourages class to think and work as a unit
5. Holds informal class discussions; provides opportunities for students to see how concepts being learned are related to students' personal experiences

Curriculum related behaviors
1. Emphasizes global aspects of concepts; before beginning lesson, ensures that students understand the performance objectives; identifies generalizations and helps children apply them to particular instances
2. Personalizes curriculum; teacher relates curriculum materials to the interests and experiences of students as well as to her or his own interests
3. Humanizes curriculum; attributes human characteristics to concepts and principles
4. Uses teaching materials to elicit expression of feelings from students; helps students apply concepts for labeling their personal experiences

---

knowledge a training program can be planned to help a teacher use strategies associated with the unfamiliar style.

Teaching in the Unfamiliar Style

Our research in teacher training led to development of an approach for training teachers to use the unfamiliar cognitive style. An overview of this approach, which is but one of several possible programs to follow, is presented in the following pages.

1. Teachers were tested with the PRFT (Appendix B, pp. 133–135) and evaluated with the background variables and Teaching Strategies Observation Instruments (Appendix C, pp. 177 and 178).
2. They were then introduced to the concept of cognitive style and to factors—social and cultural—that contribute to the development of preferred and situational cognitive styles.
3. Teachers learned how to use the Child Behavior Observation Instruments to determine the cognitive style of individual children.
4. Teachers became acquainted with characteristics of curriculum, classroom environments, and teaching styles that stimulate development of field sensitivity and field independence in children.
5. Teachers were informed about the cognitive style they used in teaching situations. At this time, they also learned to use the Teaching Strategies Observation Instruments to assess themselves and other teachers.
6. The teachers, with the help of a consultant, wrote lesson plans based on performance objectives using teaching strategies of the type which they had previously used less frequently.
7. The teachers presented a lesson to other teachers (role playing) or to children. The lessons were videotaped while a consultant observed.
8. Using the Field-Sensitive and Field-Independent Teaching Strategies Observation Instruments, the consultant and teacher evaluated the lesson.

As the teachers achieved success with the strategies, other lessons and strategies were chosen and the procedure repeated until most of the strategies in both styles were being used effectively.

Curricula and Classroom Environment

Without carefully planned curricula and classroom environments it is impossible for a teacher to function in both cognitive modes. Our observations show that most classroom environments are not conducive to bicognitive development in children: They usually are conducive only to development of field independence. Curriculum,

TABLE 7.5

Characteristics of Field-Sensitive and Field-Independent Curricula

Field-sensitive curriculum[a]	Field-independent curriculum[a]
Content	Content
1. Social abstractions: Field-sensitive curriculum is humanized through use of narration, humor, drama, and fantasy. Characterized by social words and human characteristics. Focuses on lives of persons who occupy central roles in the topic of study, such as history or scientific discovery.	1. Math and science abstractions: Field-independent curriculum uses many graphs and formulae.
2. Personalized: The ethnic background of students, as well as their homes and neighborhoods, is reflected. The teacher is given the opportunity to express personal experiences and interests.	2. Impersonal: Field-independent curriculum focuses on events, places, and facts in social studies rather than personal histories.
Structure	Structure
1. Global: Emphasis is on description of wholes and generalities; the overall view or general topic is presented first. The purpose or use of the concept or skill is clearly stated using practical examples.	1. Focus on details: The details of a concept are explored followed by the global concept.
2. Rules explicit: Rules and principles are salient. (Children who prefer to learn in the field-sensitive mode are more comfortable given the rules than when asked to discover the underlying principles for themselves.)	2. Discovery: Rules and principles are discovered from the study of details; the general is discovered from the understanding of the particulars.
3. Requires cooperation with others: The curriculum is structured in such a way that children work cooperatively with peers or with the teacher in a variety of activities.	3. Requires independent activity: The curriculum requires children to work individually, minimizing interaction with others.

[a] It should be noted that each type of curriculum is designed to facilitate teaching in the corresponding teaching style.

on the other hand, seems to favor the field-independent style in certain academic areas and the field-sensitive style in others. Commercial curricula, science and math, for example, appear to be overly biased toward the field-independent style.

In order to assist the teacher in identifying the style reflected by curriculum, we have identified characteristics that promote development of each style. These characteristics are summarized in Table 7.5.

We have found that the following are characteristics of learning environments that stimulate development of a particular cognitive style—field sensitivity or field independence—in children.

Field-Sensitive Learning Environment

1. Classroom is arranged for small-group instruction: small tables, rugs, and learning centers are available. This environment permits the teacher to work closely with students.
2. Classroom environment lends itself to group projects. It is possible for the entire class or groups to work together toward common goals.
3. Rooms are personalized. They reflect the ethnic and social backgrounds and interests of the students. Their class work and personal contributions decorate the walls and other areas.

Field-Independent Learning Environment

1. Classroom is arranged for independent activities. There are learning centers where materials are immediately available to the students, requiring minimal participation by the teacher.
2. Rooms display curriculum materials, charts, and diagrams. If children's work is displayed, it consists of materials that emphasize individual achievement.

Bicognitive Learning Environment

The ideal classroom for bicognitive development is one that allows children to work on individual projects (for which learning centers should be available) and on group projects that afford close contact with the teacher and classmates. A program of study is developed for each student so that he or she has opportunity to work with both field-sensitive and field-independent peers. In this environment it would be possible for both field-sensitive and field-independent children to act as tutors. Classroom walls would be decorated with both field-sensitive and field-independent materials.

Evaluation

The effectiveness of culturally democratic educational environments in bringing about greater academic achievement can only be determined through evaluation. Yet the entire process of evaluation itself is also affected by cognitive style. That is, cognitive styles are reflected in what is tested by assessment instruments, by the manner in which the test materials are written, and also by the behavior of the tester and the atmosphere of the testing environment.

Academic Achievement

Assessment of academic achievement is particularly important because it has been shown that both structure and content of most achievement tests favor an analytic or field-independent approach to problem solving (Cohen, 1969). Moreover, the traditional approach of the tester and the structure of traditional test situations tend to depress the performance of field-sensitive children. It is necessary to develop testing instruments that reflect both cognitive styles in order to assess the extent to which children are achieving the goal of mental flexibility or bicognitive functioning.

Test Structure

Cohen (1969) has indicated that most intelligence and achievement tests favor a parts-specific, stimulus-centered, analytic mode of abstraction, and thus are biased in the direction of field independence. Instruments with a structure more consonant with the field-sensitive cognitive style must be devised. These should emphasize global characteristics of concepts and the deductive approach to problem solving.

Test Content

Cohen (1969) has also shown that the content of achievement tests tends to favor the field-independent cognitive style. It is necessary, then, to construct instruments the content of which reflects more field sensitivity. Items, for example, should contain social material—human faces and social words. In addition, to capitalize on the "self-centered" (Cohen, 1969) orientation of field-sensitive subjects, test items should contain ethnic as well as other personalized material that is meaningful to the children being assessed.

Behavior of the Tester

Konstadt and Forman (1965) have shown that the performance of field-sensitive children is enhanced when testers indicate approval through praise by remarking, "This is a very bright group, you are going to do well on this test," or "You certainly have caught on faster than most children, I can see you will do well [p. 491]." Conversely, the performance of field-sensitive children is depressed when testers indicate disapproval: "This doesn't seem like the kind of group that can do well, but you might as well try as long as you're here," or "You're not as fast as our other groups, don't you want to cooperate [p. 491]?"

Our own research has shown that field-sensitive children do best when they are familiar with the examiner, when the examiner gives encouragement and support, and when he interprets test performance as achievement for the entire group or class. On the other hand, the performance of field-independent children is enhanced when the tester encourages individual competition. It is advisable, then, to train testers to administer tests in both the field-sensitive and field-independent modes.

Testing Environment and Test Atmosphere

Observations of field-sensitive and field-independent children in different testing situations have revealed that field-sensitive children perform best when testing is done in small groups (six to eight children). This is advantageous to field-sensitive children in two ways:

(1) it facilitates use of the field-sensitive teaching strategies; and (2) it helps to eliminate a major cause of depressed test performance in field-sensitive children—insufficient understanding of test instructions. We have observed that many field-sensitive children are reluctant to ask questions and thus frequently take a test without completely understanding what is expected of them. Testing in small groups allows for more extensive explanation of instructions and also allows the tester to identify those children who need additional explanation of instructions and practice with sample items before proceeding with the test.

It is interesting to note that children who are field independent sometimes perform poorly because of insufficient understanding of test instructions. We have observed that these children are often so impatient to begin the test that they frequently do not listen attentively to instructions. Small-group testing, then, can be beneficial to both field-independent and field-sensitive children.

Assessment, teacher training, curricula, classroom environments, and evaluation should all be directed toward the goal of achieving bicognitive functioning in children. How is this goal best accomplished? And what, specifically, are the characteristics of a bicognitive child?

Bicognitive Functioning

Stimulating Development of Bicognitive Functioning in Children

We have found the following approach to be most effective in implementing the cognitive-styles component of culturally democratic educational environments and for encouraging development of bicognition in children.

1. Teachers, teacher aides, and children are evaluated with the observation instruments at the beginning of the school year.
2. Three student groups are initially established in each classroom (an extreme field-independent group, a middle group, and an extreme field-sensitive group) based on cognitive profiles.

3. Teachers and teacher aides are given inservice training which introduces them to teaching in the unfamiliar style (see pp. 140–141).

4. Cognitive styles of teachers, teacher aides, and children are assessed throughout the year. There is also evaluation of academic achievement of students. When a consultant assigned to the classroom and the teacher or teacher's aide decide that a certain child is ready to be introduced to another style, the child is moved to another group. Children in the extreme field-sensitive or field-independent group are moved to the middle group on the first rotation. From there, children are transferred to either the extreme field-sensitive or field-independent groups.

5. As teachers and teacher aids become proficient in teacher in both styles, grouping of children becomes more flexible.

Children Developing Bicognitive Functioning

Throughout a school year the behavior of pupils of those teachers who had been given training in cognitive styles was continually evaluated. At the end of the year, teachers reviewed their accumulated evaluations and wrote brief reports on the behavior and changes in behavior of each child. Following are reports of children who demonstrated ability to function in the unfamiliar style.

1. In the fall, C was in the field-sensitive group. He was very warm, and told me a lot about his family and home life. While he was in this group, he did fine in math and reading. He liked to work with the other children, especially when he could show them how to do things.

When I put him in the middle group, he seemed to adjust quite easily. At first it was difficult for him to work by himself, but after about 3 weeks, he didn't seem to mind. He also seemed to become more competitive—at least it seemed like doing better than the other children was more important to him.

It seemed, too, that when working alone he could concentrate much better; he could ignore what was going on around him more. He seemed able to learn curriculum which was written in a field-in-

dependent manner more readily than before. In some ways, however, he remained very field sensitive, volunteering to help his classmates and looking for approval from the aides and myself whenever he did something right.

2. L was initially very field sensitive. He was very attached to my aide, Mrs. _____, and always went out of his way to help others. When I first transferred him to the field-independent group, he was visibly uncomfortable. He would hold back and refuse to participate in class discussions. At the end of the first week, he had gained more self-confidence but even then when the aide asked a question to which he knew the answer, he would begin to raise his hand but then suddenly put it down again. After 2 weeks of participating in the field-independent group, he was comfortable about the competitive atmosphere. He could become completely absorbed in his work when he had to and he demonstrated more self-confidence in solving problems presented in a field-independent style.

3. Of all the children in my classroom, J showed the least change of all. He is very field independent, but I moved him directly to the extreme field-sensitive group because I thought he was flexible and self-confident enough to make the adjustment. But he never quite became completely involved with the field-sensitive group. He seemed to be merely making the best of a bad situation, so I had to move him back to the field-independent group. While he was in the field-sensitive group, he mostly kept to himself. He seemed to regard the other kids with disdain and never participated in tasks with them. He kept complaining that they were cheating because they worked cooperatively. Now that I think about it, I recognize that the change was too drastic for him. I think I should have placed him in the middle group first. Perhaps he would have felt less threatened there.

Bicognitive Children

As we observed children in the classroom, and particularly as we observed them in the different groups, we identified certain children who appeared to be more bicognitive than most of their classmates. We studied some of these children intensively.

The following was taken from one teacher's report on a child who seemed better able than most children to function bicognitively. Our observations of this profile follow the report.

At the beginning of the year, L seemed to be very field independent. She was very competitive. She would select a child in the group and then compete with him or her. She could completely ignore other children when she was working on a test or a class assignment. She was constantly worried because she thought other children might be doing better. Whenever she finished an assignment first, she would throw her hands up and say, "I beat you, I beat you. I'm ahead of everyone."

However, her interest in forming friendships and in the humanistic aspects of curriculum made her different from the other field-independent children. Also, she sought to be physically close to me and my aides, wanting our approval whenever she succeeded at something.

Her attempts to form friendships with the other kids were not completely successful at first. This was due to the fact that she would usually behave too competitively in the games they played. The other kids wouldn't like this. But she persisted in seeking them out and eventually learned to play without feeling like she had to win.

L also showed more versatility than the other kids when she adjusted more rapidly and smoothly to the new group. She adjusted rapidly to the extreme field-sensitive group. On her first day with the field-sensitive group, however, she was alarmed by the fact that the kids were helping each other with their work. She said, "Teacher, they're cheating, they're cheating." Before long, however, she started helping the other children and enjoying the group. She was also very attracted by the humanized characteristics of the field-sensitive curriculum and adjusted quickly to the deductive presentation of the curriculum.

Even though she learned to behave field sensitively in many groups, she retained many of her field-independent behaviors. When we would give tests, she would behave like a field independent, resuming her competitiveness and ignoring what was going on around her. She is very versatile; she is able to behave according to the situation she is in at the moment.

Her versatility shows up in her classwork as well. She does well in all subjects. She is at the top of the class.

In attempting to help children become bicognitive, we have observed that certain field-independent and field-sensitive behaviors are unadaptive for optimum performance in the classroom. We have also observed that certain field-independent and field-sensitive behaviors are more critical than others to academic achievement and adjustment to the social environment of the classroom that is oriented toward development of bicognitive functioning.

Field-independent behaviors which seem to be unadaptive include: (1) excessive concern with rivalrous behavior (this often results in demeaning the performance of peers); (2) excessive concern with doing things independently (frequently children are so concerned with showing others that they can do things without help that they do not listen to instructions).

Field-sensitive behaviors which seem to be unadaptive are: (1) overattention to the social atmosphere and actions of the classroom (this sometimes interferes with the student's concentration on a task); and (2) overreliance on teacher's approval for good performance in class (this keeps the child from doing well when social reinforcement from the teacher is not immediately forthcoming).

Our research has also identified certain specific behaviors of each cognitive style that promote success in our bicognitive classrooms.

Field-independent behaviors which promote success include: (1) individual competition; (2) ability to work independently on tasks; (3) use of the discovery approach in learning; and (4) ability to deal with math and science abstractions.

Field-sensitive behaviors which promote success are: (1) ability to work cooperatively; (2) sensitivity to the feelings of peers; (3) sensitivity to a wide variety of cues; and (4) learning by modeling and imitation.

Summary

Bicognitive functioning is the most important goal of the cognitive-styles component of culturally democratic educational environments. It is especially important for Mexican American children, not only because cognitive flexibility offers them more approaches to successful academic work, but also because functioning effectively in two cognitive styles allows them to participate more fully in both the Mexican American and mainstream American cultures, helping them to achieve a bicultural identity.

References

Cohen, R. A. Conceptual styles, culture conflict and nonverbal tests of intelligence. *American Anthropologist,* 1969, **71,** 828–856.

Konstadt, N., & Forman, E. Field dependence and external directedness. *Journal of Personality and Social Psychology,* 1965, **1,** 490–493.

8

Bicognitive Development and Educational Policy

The New Concept of Bicognitive Development

Our research on *bicultural* children led us to the discovery that children who could cope effectively with the demands of *two* cultures were those children who exhibited some capacity to be able to perform within both field-sensitive and field-independent cognitive styles. This finding led us to posit a concept of bicognition or bicognitive development. We have found the concepts of field-sensitive and field-independent cognitive styles useful in identifying or defining our concept of bicognitive development, which in turn has been useful to us in our effort to bring new understanding to the rapidly developing field of bilingual, bicultural education.

Interest in the phenomenon represented by our concept of bicognition or bicognitive development has origins in antiquity. The early Chinese philosophers, for example, concerned with the duality of the human personality, described two forces, Yin and Yang, corresponding to the female and male components which were believed to reside in each individual. The ideal human development is conceived as having been attained when the two components of Yin and Yang are equally well developed and are in balance with one another within the individual. The mystery of the duality of the human personality also intrigued the well-known writer, Virginia Woolf, who in a series of lectures in the 1920s, referred to Coleridge's concept of the "androgynous mind." Woolf's thoughts (see A Room of One's Own), like the concept of Yin and Yang, center on the possibility that both female and male "minds" exist together in the brain of each human being. One of the important contributions of our work is an effort to bring such thinking within the arena of the social sciences and education for the possible insights it offers to increased understanding of the development of the human personality and its implications for educational policy and planning.

Bicognitive development offers a fresh vantage point from which an issue of long standing in the field of education can be viewed. Argument has existed in the field of education between those who believe that the cognitive domain should be emphasized over the affective domain and those who insist that the affective domain should be given higher priority in the determination of educational goals. By focusing on bicognitive development, however, the bipolar delineation of characteristics according to affective or cognitive domain becomes irrelevant. Competent and effective functioning in both cognitive styles implies integration and equal development of the affective and cognitive domains. The goal that children become more versatile and adaptable to the increasingly complex demands of life in a postindustrial society may be reached by helping them develop the ability to switch cognitive styles—to be cognitive "switch-hitters"—or to draw upon both styles at any given time.

Bicognitive Development and Psychological Theory

We believe that our concept of bicognitive development can be a guiding concept in the field of psychology, particularly that branch concerned with child development and its role in educational planning. This concept is particularly pertinent to cognitive-development theory and psychological and educational testing.

One interpretation of the rather lopsided emphasis on the field-independent cognitive style points out the compatibility of field independence with the demands of Western industrial society. This interpretation might account for the popularity of Piaget's theories of cognitive development in American psychology. This narrow view of cognitive development, which may indeed reflect the values of a technologically oriented society, is perhaps no better seen than in Witkin's (Witkin, Dyke, Faterson, Goodenough, & Karp, 1962) theory of psychological differentiation in which field sensitivity, in contrast to field independence, is considered to be the "more rudimentary form of mental development."

Assessment instruments, like theories of mental development, clearly reflect a bias that favors the field-independent cognitive style. Cohen's (1969) work has clearly shown, for example, that a number of instruments, including nonverbal tests, for assessing academic achievement as well as IQ are heavily laden with items reflecting field independence. Unfortunately, this implies to those responsible for educational planning that the field-independent mode is the only important mode of organizing, classifying, and assimilating information about the environment. Such a message misinforms educators, and impedes efforts to develop educational environments designed to stimulate bicognitive growth.

The bicognitive perspective that we have outlined can help in psychology's continued efforts to arrive at newer understanding of mental development and functioning. It clearly implies the need for a more comprehensive theory of cognitive development and new methods and techniques of assessment that reflect a broader view of human intelligence.

The Concept of Bicognitive Development and
New Understandings of Brain Specialization

Within recent years, particularly through the efforts of such writers as TenHouten (1971), Sperry (1964), and Ornstein (1973), understanding of the functions of the two cerebral hemispheres has taken an unusual and interesting turn. Evidence strongly suggests that the separate functions of each side of the brain correspond remarkably to those that have been identified with the cognitive modes of field independence and field sensitivity. This newer conception of brain specialization provides our concept of bicognitive development with a physiological referent for the potential comprehension of such phenomena as mental flexibility or cognitive switching. At the risk of appearing facetious, it also provides us with the opportunity to express anew what we believe to be the field-independent orientation in American public education: American public education has tended to develop one hemisphere of the brain at the expense of the other.

The new frontiers that studies of brain specialization, cognitive styles, and bicognition have opened for research make even greater the need for interdisciplinary collaboration among professionals. Increasingly broader circles of psychological and scientific communities must become involved. Moreover, there is now sufficient empirical and theoretical evidence to warrant the closer collaboration of educators with other professionals who are specialists in the physiology and psychology of brain functioning. Some of this evidence is based on observations of the salutary effects of bilingualism. Bilingual/bicultural education should be understood as profoundly beneficial to all children, rather than to select groups alone. Bicognitive development implies that educational policies and practices must enhance the ability of American public education to distribute its educational resources for the greater good.

Bicognitive Development and Education in a Pluralistic Society

The exclusive focus on the field-independent cognitive mode in public education has had many deleterious consequences. Among these, two are outstanding. On the one hand, it has denied equal access to educational resources to children whose preferred cognitive style is field sensitive. On the other hand, the development of children who are field independent has been restricted by the continued development of this style at the expense of the field-sensitive mode. (Considering these observations along with the recent research on brain specialization, we cannot resist a pun: Public education's efforts to educate the "whole child" appear to be halfwitted.)

The struggle for pluralism must be seen in a broad context: The development of culturally democratic educational environments is the concern of all Americans. The role of bicognitive development must be made a decision-making factor in educational policy and planning at every level of concern.

The concept of bicognitive development can help to make public education more effective in assisting all Americans to develop their personalities to the fullest and to learn to live in harmony with one another.

References

Cohen, R. A. Conceptual styles, culture conflict and nonverbal tests of intelligence. *American Anthropologist,* 1969, **71,** 828–856.

Ornstein, R. E. Right and left thinking. *Psychology Today,* 1973, **6**(12), 86–92.

Sperry, R. W. The great cerebral commissure. *Scientific American,* 1964, **210**(1), 42–52.

TenHouten, W. D. Cognitive styles and social order. Final Report, Part II. O. E. O. Study Nonr B00-5135, "Thought, race, and opportunity." Los Angeles, California: University of California, 1971.

Witkin, H. A., Dyk, R. B., Faterson, H. F., Goodenough, D. R., & Karp, S. A. *Psychological differentiation.* New York: Wiley, 1962.

Woolf, V. *A room of one's own.* (12th Impression.) London: Hogarth Press, 1954.

APPENDIX A

The School Situations
Picture Stories Technique

The School Situations Picture Stories Technique (SSPST) is an instrument similar to the Thematic Apperception Test. It is designed to assess motivation and conflict in elementary school children (ages 9–11).

The SSPST consists of a set of seven line drawings of a person(s) in a setting related to education.

Administration

Children are tested individually. They are presented with one card at a time in the following order: (1) student and teacher, (2) student and mother, (3) student and father, (4) two students of the same ethnic group, (5) two students—one Mexican American and the other non-Mexican American, (6) student, parents, and principal, and (7) student studying alone. The child is asked to tell a story to each picture. He is encouraged to tell the most interesting story he can. In composing the story he is asked to answer three questions: (1) What is happening? (2) What happened before? (3) How will the story end?

Scoring for Assessment of Motivation

An abbreviated version of the scoring system devised by McClelland and his colleagues[1] is used for assessment of motivation. A maximum of four points can be given for each story. One point can be given for each of the following categories: (1) *imagery*—reference made in the story to a particular motive or to a goal related to a particular motive such as achievement, affiliation, aggression, etc. (e.g., Juan wants to become a lawyer); (2) *instrumental activity*—any activity independent of the original statement indicating that the character in the story is doing something to obtain the goal associated with the motive (e.g., Juan studies very hard so that he can enter law school); (3) *positive outcome of instrumental activity*—activity leads to the achievement of the goal (e.g., Juan is admitted to law school); and (4) *thema*—the plot of the story revolves around a particular motive (e.g., Juan's desire to become a lawyer).

Of special importance in assessing need achievement in Mexican American children are achievement for the family and cooperative achievement. The scoring categories for achievement for the family are as follows: (1) *achievement imagery*—character in the story is trying to achieve a goal for the purpose of benefiting his family or making his family proud of him (e.g., Ricardo wants his parents to be proud of him, or Ricardo wants to become an engineer and make a lot of money so that he can put his brothers and sisters through school); (2) *instrumental activity*—any activity independent of the original statement that helps the character in the story achieve for his family (e.g., Ricardo studies very hard); (3) *positive outcome of instrumental activity*—instrumental activity leads to the achievement of the goal (e.g., Ricardo makes A's in all his courses and his parents are very proud of him); and (4) *achievement thema*—achievement for the family is central plot or theme of the story.

[1] McClelland, D. C., Atkinson, J. W., Clark, R. A., & Lowell, E. L. *The achievement motive.* New York: Appleton-Century-Croft, 1953.

The scoring categories for cooperative achievement are: (1) *achievement imagery*—the character in the story is working toward a goal in cooperation with others, such as a team effort (e.g., Roberto wants his team to be champs in the league); (2) *instrumental activity*—any activity independent of the original statement that helps to achieve cooperatively (e.g., Roberto gives encouragement to the members of his team); (3) *positive outcome of instrumental activity*—the effect of the instrumental activity leads to achievement of the goal (e.g., Roberto's team wins the championship); (4) *achievement thema*—cooperative achievement is central plot of theme of the story.

Scoring for Conflicts

The SSPST is also used to assess intrapsychic and psychosocial conflicts. Conflict is defined as a state of anxiety or tension resulting when two or more forces are in opposition. Conflict can be intrapsychic (the forces in conflict are within the person) or psychosocial (only one of the forces is within the person).

Total conflict score.   The total number of intrapsychic or psychosocial conflicts that occur in all seven stories.

Cause of conflicts.   The cause of the conflict mentioned in the stories is identified. Of particular interest with Mexican American children is determination of the number of conflicts that are the result of value differences, that is, differences between the student's values and those of school personnel, teachers, peers, or parents. Of interest in analyzing psychosocial conflicts is determination of the particular person or institution with whom most conflicts occur.

The information derived from scoring for conflict is helpful in determining counseling needs of Mexican American students, and in preventing possible conflict between Mexican American and non-Mexican American students, or between Mexican American students and school personnel. It is also useful in identifying those aspects of the educational environment that need to be changed in order to eliminate problems and conflicts.

Instruments Most Frequently
Used for Assessing Cognitive
Styles: Special Implications for
Mexican American Children

Portable Rod and Frame Test

The Portable Rod and Frame Test (PRFT) consists of a translucent, polyethelene plastic box. The box rests on a table, and the child is asked to position his head at one end of the box. The child's view, as a result of this position, is restricted to the interior of the box. He sees directly in front of him a black frame and a black rod—each of which can be turned independently (see Figure 4.5, p. 69). The examiner raises a curtain in front of the subject's eyes, so that the rod and frame are no longer in view, and then moves the rod and frame 28° off the vertical. He lowers the curtain and asks the subject to tell him the direction in which to move the rod in order to return it to its vertical position. He warns the subject that the frame will remain tilted. Subjects are given eight trials in the following order: F(frame) L(left) 28°, R(rod) L 28°; FL 28°, RR(right) 28°; FR 28°,

RR 28°; FR 28°, RL 28°; FL 28°, RL 28°; FL 28°, FR 28°, RR 28°; FR 28°, RL 28°. The subject's score is the average number of degrees of deviation of the rod from the vertical for the eight trials given. A lower score is indicative of greater field independence while a higher score indicates less field independence.

The instructions for the PRFT are simple and can easily be translated into Spanish for those Mexican American children whose primary language is Spanish. Also, children are not likely to view the PRFT as a test and become inhibited. Since there are no obvious "right" or "wrong" answers, it is unlikely that the child will become discouraged by "failures."

There are, however, several disadvantages to the PRFT which should be considered. Some young children have difficulty comprehending the concept of vertical. (Care should be taken to ensure that this concept is clearly understood before administration is begun.) Moreover, some children are intimidated by the size of the instrument itself. In addition, our observations seem to show that the PRFT does not appear to assess field sensitivity or bicognitive functioning.

Children's Embedded Figures Test

The Children's Embedded Figures Test (CEFT) consists of two sets of complex geometric figures. The task for the child is to find a particular simple geometric figure in each of the complex figures (see Figure 4.3, p. 68). In one set a triangle is the simple figure which is hidden in the complex figure. In the other set, the simple figure is the shape of a house. There are 11 complex figure cards (tent series) and 14 complex figure cards (house series).

The test is individually administered. The examiner first shows the child the simple geometric figure, then one at a time the corresponding series of complex figures. The child is asked to find the triangle hidden within each complex figure. This procedure is repeated with the house series.

The child's score is the sum of correct responses for both the tent and house series. A higher score is indicative of a field-independent cognitive style and a lower score indicates a less field-independent cognitive style.

While the CEFT is commonly used among children there are no specific advantages in using this test with Mexican American children. There are, however, disadvantages. Some children are threatened by the format of the CEFT because of the resemblance to intelligence and achievement tests with which they may have had negative experiences. Second, if a child is unable to locate the simple figure in a few of the cards, he may become discouraged and give up.

Draw-a-Person Test

The Draw-a-Person Test (DAPT) has also been used for assessment of cognitive style. In this test the child is given a sheet of plain white paper and a pencil and is instructed to draw a whole person. Upon completion of this drawing, the child is given a second sheet of paper and is told to draw a person of the opposite sex from the one he just drew.

Each drawing is evaluated according to a "sophistication-of-the-body-concept"[1] scale that was designed to reflect the degree of sophistication of drawn figures. A rating scale of 1 (most sophisticated) to 5 (least sophisticated) is used for each drawing. The total score (sum of scores on both drawings) is used as the indicator of cognitive style. A lower score indicates greater field independence while a higher score is indicative of less field independence.

One primary advantage of the DAPT for Mexican American children is that the instructions are simple and can be easily translated into Spanish. The other advantage is that the DAPT does not resemble achievement or intelligence tests.

There is no specific disadvantage to the DAPT in assessing Mexican American children, but accurate scoring does require considerable training. Witkin (personal communication) has observed that inexperienced scorers tend to be unduly influenced by clothing, thus sometimes assigning inflated scores to figures with elaborate clothing details.

[1] Witkin H. A., Dyk, R. B., Faterson, H. F., Goodenough, D. R., & Karp, S. A. *Psychological differentiation.* New York: Wiley, 1962. Pp. 118–133.

Field-Sensitive/Field-Independent Behavior Observation Instruments: Child and Teacher

Child

The Field-Sensitive and Field-Independent Behavior Observation Instruments, which are included in the following pages, are designed to assess children's overall or preferred cognitive style as well as to determine "situation-specific" modes of functioning. That is, a child may well be predominantly field sensitive, but in certain situations he may behave in a field-independent manner. Moreover, these instruments used together allow the teacher or investigator to determine the degree to which a child may be bicognitive, as well as plan a program to increase the child's cognitive flexibility.

The ratings indicate the frequencies with which certain behaviors are used and determine a preferred cognitive style. A rating scale of 5 (almost always) to 1 (never) is used for each behavior. Observations are made of a child's behavior in a wide variety of situations over several days. The situation-specific rating, however, follows from observations made of the child functioning in one particular setting. The situation-specific ratings are most useful in helping plan an individualized program for the child.

Ratings obtained for the preferred cognitive style of a first-grade girl appear on the next two pages, followed by a short discussion of how a teacher would use this information in preparing a program to help her function bicognitively.

CHILD RATING FORM
FIELD-SENSITIVE OBSERVABLE BEHAVIORS

Instructions: Evaluate the child for each behavior listed below by placing a check in the appropriate column.

An example
_____   _____   _____   _____
Child's Name   Grade   School   Date

_____
Observer's Name

Global
Situation (e.g., "Math lesson"); for general or overall rating, write "Global"

FIELD-SENSITIVE OBSERVABLE BEHAVIORS	FREQUENCY				
	NOT TRUE	SELDOM TRUE	SOMETIMES TRUE	OFTEN TRUE	ALMOST ALWAYS TRUE
RELATIONSHIP TO PEERS					
1. Likes to work with others to achieve a common goal.					X
2. Likes to assist others.				X	
3. Is sensitive to feelings and opinions of others.					X
PERSONAL RELATIONSHIP TO TEACHER					
1. Openly expresses positive feelings for teacher.				X	
2. Asks questions about teacher's tastes and personal experiences; seeks to become like teacher.				X	
INSTRUCTIONAL RELATIONSHIP TO TEACHER					
1. Seeks guidance and demonstration from teacher.			X		
2. Seeks rewards which strengthen relationship with teacher.					X
3. Is highly motivated when working individually with teacher.					X
CHARACTERISTICS OF CURRICULUM WHICH FACILITATE LEARNING					
1. Performance objectives and global aspects of curriculum are carefully explained.				X	
2. Concepts are presented in humanized or story format.				X	
3. Concepts are related to personal interests and experiences of children.				X	

169

CHILD RATING FORM
FIELD-INDEPENDENT OBSERVABLE BEHAVIORS

Instructions: Evaluate the child for each behavior listed below by placing a check in the appropriate column.

An example
_____   _____   _____   _____
Child's Name   Grade   School   Date

_____
Observer's Name

Global
_____
Situation: (e.g., "Math lesson"); for general or overall rating, write "Global"

FIELD-INDEPENDENT OBSERVABLE BEHAVIORS	FREQUENCY				
	NOT TRUE	SELDOM TRUE	SOMETIMES TRUE	OFTEN TRUE	ALMOST ALWAYS TRUE
RELATIONSHIP TO PEERS					
1. Prefers to work independently.		X			
2. Likes to compete and gain individual recognition.	X				
3. Task oriented; is inattentive to social environment when working.		X			
PERSONAL RELATIONSHIP TO TEACHER					
1. Rarely seeks physical contact with teacher.	X				
2. Formal: interactions with teacher are restricted to tasks at hand.	X				
INSTRUCTIONAL RELATIONSHIP TO TEACHER					
1. Likes to try new tasks without teacher's help.			X		
2. Impatient to begin tasks; likes to finish first.		X			
3. Seeks nonsocial rewards.	X				
CHARACTERISTICS OF CURRICULUM WHICH FACILITATE LEARNING					
1. Details of concepts are emphasized: parts have meaning of their own.		X			
2. Deals well with math and science concepts.	X				
3. Based on discovery approach.	X				

170

Planning Strategies for Developing
Bicognitive Functioning: An Example

The ratings obtained with the Field-Sensitive and Field-Independent Child Observation Instruments shown on pp. 169 and 170 indicate that this child is predominantly field sensitive. By using the scores from these two rating forms, a program can be planned to help the child become bicognitive.

The overall impression the ratings offer is that the child needs to be introduced to successful functioning in the field-independent cognitive style. Since most school environments are oriented toward field-independent learning, it is quite possible that this child has already been exposed to field-independent learning situations, and, since she remains field sensitive, may have experienced difficulty. It is critical, therefore, that success and approval be designed into the field-independent situations to which she is introduced. Field-sensitive teaching strategies and rewards should be used in a manner that encourages or elicits field-independent behaviors (see the following). Field-independent situations or tasks should be brief at first, then gradually lengthened. Such tasks should also be simple at first—ones that deal with concepts the child has already mastered, and only gradually made more difficult. Finally, it is wisest to concentrate on one area of field-independent functioning at a time, moving to another area when the child demonstrates that she is fairly comfortable using field-independent behavior to which she has been introduced earlier.

Relationship to Peers

FIELD-SENSITIVE OBSERVABLE BEHAVIORS

1. *Likes to work with others to achieve a common goal* ------- 5
2. *Likes to assist others* -- 4
3. *Is sensitive to the feelings and opinions of others* ------------- 5

FIELD-INDEPENDENT OBSERVABLE BEHAVIORS

1. *Prefers to work alone* -- 2
2. *Likes to compete and gain individual recognition* ----------- 1

3. *Task oriented, is inattentive to social environment when working* --- 2

This child does not enjoy working alone. She would rather help others than compete with them, and is sensitive to their needs and feelings. She also has difficulty focusing on a task when other things are happening around her. Learning to work alone and to participate in competitive situations should increase task orientation. Therefore, focusing on the first and second field-independent behaviors should improve functioning in the third area, task orientation.

Working alone. In introducing the child to working by herself, assign tasks that can be completed quickly and easily, tasks that the child can accomplish with minimal assistance or which perhaps review concepts she has already mastered. Introduce the task carefully, on a one-to-one basis if possible, then indicate that it is important to you that she do this work by herself. Set her to work in an area of the classroom with minimal distractions. When the child has completed an assignment alone, personalized praise should be immediately forthcoming so that the child associates praise from the teacher (a field-sensitive incentive) with working alone.

Competition. The ratings indicate that this student needs some experience in competitive situations. Again, success must be designed as part of the activity while introducing competitive situations. Personalization can be used to facilitate participation in competitive activities: "I will be very proud of you if you do this well." Introduce her to competing with herself: "Last week you could do these problems in 15 minutes. Let's see if you can do them in 10 minutes today."

Task orientation. If competition and working alone have been successfully introduced, the child will no doubt be more task oriented. Continue to focus her attention on assigned tasks. It may be helpful to point out time factors: "We want to finish this and have it all correct before we go to . . . ."

Personal Relationship to Teacher

FIELD-SENSITIVE OBSERVABLE BEHAVIORS

1. *Openly expresses positive feelings for teacher* ---------------- 4
2. *Asks questions about teacher's tastes and personal experiences; seeks to become like teacher* ----------------------- 4

FIELD-INDEPENDENT OBSERVABLE BEHAVIORS

1. *Rarely seeks physical contact with teacher* -------------------- 1
2. *Formal; interactions with teacher are limited to tasks at hand* 1

The behaviors of this category are concerned with the role that the teacher–child relationship plays in the learning process.

The implication of working toward bicognitive functioning in this area is not to change the child's preference in style of relating to her teacher, but rather to accept behaviors from the teacher that ordinarily discourage the field-sensitive child. From the standpoint of helping this child learn to function in the field-independent cognitive style, the goal here is directly related to task orientation. Provide situations in which your participation is more formal and in which the child's participation is focused on the materials or task rather than on you. Be sure to exercise caution that the child is not given the impression that you are no longer interested in her. In order to maintain the bicognitive atmosphere it is important to follow these activities with a field-sensitive activity in which your relationship with her is closer.

Instructional Relationship to Teacher

FIELD-SENSITIVE OBSERVABLE BEHAVIORS

1. *Seeks guidance and demonstration from teacher* ----------- 3
2. *Seeks rewards which strengthen relationship with teacher* --- 5
3. *Is highly motivated when working individually with teacher* 5

FIELD-INDEPENDENT OBSERVABLE BEHAVIORS

1. *Likes to try new tasks without teacher's help* ---------------- 3
2. *Impatient to begin tasks; likes to finish first* ------------------ 2
3. *Seeks nonsocial rewards* --- 1

The fact that this child occasionally likes to try things "on her own" offers a starting point for encouraging field independence in this area. Even though she performs best when working on a one-to-one basis with you, try steering her away from this situation to a more field-independent method of study. Try assigning a particular task, explaining the task well on an individual basis, and then leaving the child to work alone or at a table with a few other children. Eventually, you might distribute work that is self-explanatory and let her proceed by herself. Remember that the assigned work must be within the child's grasp so she does not become discouraged. A hug, a pat on the shoulder, or the wink of an eye before you move away could provide the necessary incentive for her to continue doing her best work on her own. After using this approach a few times, personalized rewards could be interspersed with nonsocial rewards. When first attempting to motivate the child with nonsocial rewards, tell her that these rewards were important to you when you were in school. That is, personalize the child's introduction to these incentives or rewards.

Characteristics of Curriculum
Which Facilitate Learning

FIELD-SENSITIVE OBSERVABLE BEHAVIORS

1. *Performance objectives and global aspects of curriculum are carefully explained* -- 4
2. *Concepts are presented in humanized or story format* ------ 4
3. *Concepts are related to personal interests and experiences of children* --- 4

FIELD-INDEPENDENT OBSERVABLE BEHAVIORS

1. *Details of concepts are emphasized; parts have meaning of their own* --- 2

2. *Deals with math and science concepts* ------------------------ *1*
3. *Based on discovery approach* ------------------------------------- *1*

Although the child demonstrates a preference for field-sensitive curriculum, she must be introduced to field-independent curriculum to which she will undoubtedly be exposed throughout her later school years. Again, in introducing the child to the field-independent curriculum, care must be exercised to ensure the child's initial interest and success. Introduce field-independent lessons and materials with field-sensitive teaching strategies. For example, introduce curriculum with math abstractions in a cooperative setting and afterward give field-sensitive rewards.

Teacher

On pages 177 and 178 are Teaching Strategies Observation Instruments designed to assess the cognitive mode of a teacher's presentations and classroom behaviors. These instruments are used for two distinct purposes: (1) to identify an overall preferred teaching style, and (2) to evaluate the teaching style used in a particular lesson or situation.

The purpose of identifying an overall teaching style is to give the teacher an idea of which areas of classroom functioning need to be developed, practiced, or utilized. The ratings given in an overall observation indicate the frequencies with which certain behaviors are used. These ratings are most useful in helping a teacher evaluate his or her own teaching style. Since many variables affect an overall teaching style, including the cognitive style of the children in a particular room and the type of lesson being presented, caution should be exercised in drawing conclusions from these overall ratings. That is, the ratings reflect frequencies, not ability, and a low frequency should not be assumed to indicate that a teacher necessarily needs specific training in these areas.

The observation instrument is most valuable in teacher training when used to evaluate a particular lesson or situation that is purposely given in either the field-independent or field-sensitive mode. That is, a teacher plans and presents a lesson in one cognitive style, and is then evaluated to determine his or her success in utilizing that cognitive style in the classroom. Following these observations, training would reflect consideration of the teacher's scores on these lesson presentations.

The sample Observation Instruments that appear on the next two pages include the overall ratings that a teacher gave himself in evaluating his own teaching. Based on this self-evaluation, the teacher initiated a self-training program to practice behaviors that he rated as occuring with less frequency. Shortly thereafter, the teacher presented two lessons, one field independent and one field sensitive, for the purpose of being evaluated by an outside observer. The ratings from these observations were then used to prescribe further training, including practice lessons and preparation of cognitively appropriate curriculum materials.

FIELD-INDEPENDENT TEACHING STRATEGIES
OBSERVATION INSTRUMENT

Indicate the frequency with which each teaching behavior occurs by placing a check in the appropriate column.

Teacher's Name _____

Overall

Teaching Situation

Grade _____ School _____ Date _____

Self-evaluation

Observer's Name

Teacher's intended teaching style (if applicable) _____

FIELD-INDEPENDENT TEACHING BEHAVIORS	FREQUENCY				
	NOT TRUE	SELDOM TRUE	SOMETIMES TRUE	OFTEN TRUE	ALMOST ALWAYS TRUE
PERSONAL BEHAVIORS					
1. Maintains formal relationships with students.			X		
2. Centers attention on instructional objectives: gives social atmosphere secondary importance.		X			
INSTRUCTIONAL BEHAVIORS					
1. Encourages independent student achievement.				X	
2. Encourages competition between students.			X		
3. Adopts a consultant role.		X			
4. Encourages trial and error learning.		X			
5. Encourages task orientation			X		
CURRICULUM RELATED BEHAVIORS					
1. Focuses on details of curriculum materials.				X	
2. Focuses on facts and principles; encourages using novel approaches to problem solving.				X	
3. Relies on graphs, charts and formulas.		X			
4. Emphasizes inductive learning and discovery approach.				X	

FIELD-SENSITIVE TEACHING STRATEGIES
OBSERVATION INSTRUMENT

Indicate the frequency with which each teaching behavior occurs by placing a check in the appropriate column.

| Teacher's Name | | Grade | School | Date |

Overall

Teaching Situation

Self-evaluation

Observer's Name

Teacher's intended teaching style (if applicable)

FIELD-SENSITIVE TEACHING BEHAVIORS	NOT TRUE	SELDOM TRUE	SOMETIMES TRUE	OFTEN TRUE	ALMOST ALWAYS TRUE
PERSONAL BEHAVIORS					
1. Displays physical and verbal expressions of approval and warmth.					X
2. Uses personalized rewards which strengthen the relationship with students.				X	
INSTRUCTIONAL BEHAVIORS					
1. Expresses confidence in child's ability to succeed.				X	
2. Gives guidance to students: makes purpose and main principles of lesson obvious to students.			X		
3. Encourages learning through modeling; asks children to imitate.		X			
4. Encourages cooperation and development of group feeling.				X	
5. Holds internal class discussions relating concepts to students' experiences.			X		
CURRICULUM RELATED BEHAVIORS					
1. Emphasizes global aspects of concepts; clearly explains performance objectives.	X				
2. Personalizes curriculum.				X	
3. Humanizes curriculum.				X	
4. Uses teaching materials to elicit expression of feelings from students.				X	

FREQUENCY

APPENDIX D

Recommendations for Implementing Culture-Matching Teaching Strategies

Nonverbal Indications of Acceptance

1. Take advantage of opportunities to communicate with individual children through meaningful looks, smiles, putting your arm around them.
2. Provide opportunities for children to work right next to you, particularly when you are reading a story or being read to.
3. When children are having a good laugh, do not feel reluctant to share in their laughter.

Personalizing

1. Mention personal feelings, your own likes and dislikes, to the children from time to time.

2. Tell the children things about your own life, show pictures of your family, have members of your family visit the school, perhaps at open house.

3. Take care to know things about the children: their favorite colors or foods, things they like doing or visits they enjoy. Compliment them on their appearances, new clothes, etc. Above all, be sensitive to their home backgrounds.

4. Display photographs of the children in the classroom.

5. Know and at least mention, if not celebrate, birthdays, particularly in the lower grades.

6. Lesson material should be related to personal experiences of the children whenever possible: Math stories can refer to local places. For example, mention a local store rather than referring to "the store."

7. Relate feelings mentioned in stories to the children's own feelings.

Encouraging Cooperation

1. Reward instances of helpfulness and consideration you see in the classroom with your approval. For instance, remark on how nice it is to see a child or children helping a new student.

2. Assign tasks for small groups of children to do together. Children can cooperate on doing worksheets, measuring, cleaning up or tidying, and delivering messages. Murals and wall charts also make good cooperative activities.

3. Encourage a cooperative attitude about classroom behavior. Point out that good behavior reflects on everyone in the room, particularly on the playground or when there is a substitute teacher.

4. Occasionally direct children to each other for help in their classroom work; for instance, they can ask each other how to spell words, or how to read words.

5. Cross-age cooperation can be very effective; older children should be invited to the room and the children in your room could help with younger children.

Achievement for the Family

1. Send messages to the child's family expressing pleasure with his or her achievements.
2. Remind children how proud their families will be that they can read, add, subtract.
3. Mention the child's family when you are talking about when he or she grows up. For instance, a child could be asked how his mother will feel when he or she is in the next grade, or how pleased the family will be when the child is old enough to drive them in the car.
4. Send samples of each child's work home frequently, reminding the child how pleased his mother will be to see it. Add a brief note to the work if possible.
5. Make every effort to meet families personally, and take the opportunity to express appreciation of what the families do for their children.
6. Make wall displays out of materials that children have worked on at home with their parents and brought to school.

Accepting Children's Feelings and Ideas

1. Children's contributions should be accepted, though they may occur at inopportune moments. If you cannot stop what you are doing to listen to a child, say politely that you will listen as soon as you have a moment, and *then make sure you do so.*
2. Children should be free to express their likes and dislikes about activities. You should be able to say, "I know you don't like doing this, but I want you to do it for a little while. After this, we'll do something that you like." That is, the child might have to do something, but he should not have to pretend that he likes it when he doesn't.
3. Make your feelings known to the children from time to time, your preferences, moods, etc.
4. Be sensitive to emotional upsets the children may be experi-

encing and do not pressure them to perform as usual if you know of or sense some unusual situation.

5. Accept pupils' ideas. If a child adds something relevant from his own experience, include this experience in the lesson. ("Tell me how your father knows one piece of wood is longer than another piece of wood.")

Showing Sensitivity to Appropriate Sex Roles

1. Be aware that Mexican American children from traditional communities are often conscious of sex roles, and that you could create problems for a child if you were to force that child to participate in an activity which he or she would consider inappropriate to his or her sex role.

Eliciting Modeling

1. Have children repeat words and actions after you. This is always appropriate in language-learning situations.
2. Show a child how to do things often: how to hold his pencil, mix his paints, etc.
3. Provide a model of the skills the children are learning: how to print, how to make numbers.
4. Provide a model of classroom duties: how to put your materials away, put the books away, help another person do something.
5. Do not hesitate to recognize a child who is attempting to do something the way you do it: "¡Que bien! You have drawn a flower that looks just like the one I drew."

Cultural Highlighting

1. Mention holidays that are celebrated by the local Mexican American community and hold appropriate celebrations in the classroom.
2. Bring Spanish language magazines, books, comics, and newspapers into the room.

3. Be aware of celebrations that the children in the classroom will know about: confirmations, weddings, etc.
4. Mexican Americans who are prominent in public life—sports figures, people in government, artists—should be featured in lessons and bulletin board displays.
5. Members of the local community should be invited to the classroom.
6. Refer from time to time to the extended family.

Using Spanish

1. Use Spanish informally throughout the school day for giving classroom directions, telling little stories to Spanish speakers, etc. Use Spanish diminutives and ways of addressing children (*Miguelito, hijo, niña*) and repeat Spanish folk sayings.
2. Address other adults in Spanish in order to show the children that the language has prestige among adults. Be particularly careful to address outside visitors who know Spanish in this language.
3. The daily story should often be in Spanish or at least contain some Spanish words and phrases.
4. The class should learn Spanish songs and rhymes.
5. Ask the children how to say things in Spanish. Spanish names should be pronounced correctly.

Encouraging Fantasy

1. Encourage storytelling by telling stories frequently.
2. Dramatic situations should be devised where the child acts as if he is in another situation.
3. Children should be encouraged to sympathize with each other and with people they hear about in stories ("How do you think Miguelito felt when . . .").
4. Opportunities should be provided for the children to tell stories about pictures they draw or paint.

Index

B
C 6
D 7
E 8
F 9
G 0
H 1
I 2
J 3